Citizens National Bank

CNB

Discover the Advantage

Citizens National Bank
proudly presents…
a signed edition of
the new volume entitled

EATING YOUR WAY ACROSS OHIO
101 Must Places to Eat

Enjoy Ohio's finest!

Karen A. Patterson, Author 2011

Eating Your Way Across

OHIO

Eating Your Way Across OHIO

101 MUST PLACES to EAT

Karen A. Patterson

FOREWORD BY **Gary West**

Acclaim Press™
MORLEY, MISSOURI

Acclaim Press
— Your Next Great Book —

P.O. Box 238
Morley, MO 63767
(573) 472-9800
www.acclaimpress.com

Designer: M. Frene Melton
Cover Design: M. Frene Melton

Library of Congress Cataloging-in-Publication Data

Patterson, Karen A.
  Eating Your Way Across Ohio: 101 Must Place to Eat / Karen A. Patterson.
    p. cm.
  Includes index.
  ISBN-13: 978-1-935001-83-6 (alk. paper)
  ISBN-10: 1-935001-83-3 (alk. paper)
  1. Restaurants--Ohio--Guidebooks. I. Title.
  TX907.3.O3P38 2011
  647.95771--dc23
                        2011035512

First Printing: 2011
Printed in the United States of America
10 9 8 7 6 5 4 3 2 1

Contents

Introduction

Eating Your Way Across Ohio: 101 Must Places to Eat is a wonderful chance to showcase the best restaurants in Ohio. Our state is not only significant from a politically strategic position, but it is a great place to live and eat. It offers diversity in the topography of the land, a variety of unique sites to visit, a mixture of entertainment options, a range of educational opportunities, a strong multi-cultural influence, and thousands of restaurants. Selecting only 101 from the many good eateries was difficult, but I selected the best to be included here. A couple ranked five stars, but most were exceptional diners, cafes and small establishments that serve down home, good food at reasonable prices in a comfortable atmosphere.

This book is designed to be a guide for those residents who want to enjoy a great meal not too far from home, as well as for those who are visiting our fine state. Each restaurant was evaluated based on the same criteria: the quality and price of the food, atmosphere, location, cleanliness of the facility (including the restrooms), the attentiveness of the staff, and, most importantly, locally owned. I did not include corporate fast food restaurants or franchises which are prevalent in our society and feature predictable menus. And, finally, no restaurant in this book paid to be included. The selection was based on my experience and the criteria.

When I began my research, area Chambers of Commerce and Visitors Bureaus all over the state, even other restaurant owners and managers, referred me to places that they thought were worthy of being reviewed. Family, friends and at times strangers offered their recommendations by sharing what their favorite spots were and what they particularly enjoyed.

The mountain of research material kept growing as my assistant, Jolinda Van Dyke, and I scoped out each of the 88 counties and charted our course. Often an establishment was just what I expected when I arrived, but at times it missed the mark based on some element of the criteria. If I did not feel comfortable there, I would not recommend it. So my quest for finding the best Ohio eateries was challenging in that quality in all categories was essential.

I personally visited every restaurant, sampled their food and determined whether you, the reader, would enjoy visiting that particular place, and especially whether it was family friendly. However, at times I had a travelling companion that included Jolinda, my husband John, or my good friend

Karen Raybould. Whether alone or with someone else, I travelled over 7,000 miles around the state and enjoyed every minute of it.

Though there are numerous types of eating establishments – bed & breakfasts, bistros, brasseries, buffets, cafés, delis, diners, drive-ins, grilles/grills, inns, lounges, pubs, ristorantes, roadhouses, saloons, steakhouses, taverns, and wineries – each have their own trademark dishes unique menus offering a specific selection of food consistent with their theme. With the diversified eating preferences of most Americans, there is an eatery that will serve the perfect dish to match your specific taste. The challenge is finding it and I hope this book will help.

Those who are associated with restaurants, whether they are owners, managers, chefs or servers, are dedicated to the mission of creating an atmosphere for the satisfaction and comfort of others. They often work long hours, sometimes without a day off for weeks including holidays. They are on their feet all day, with logistical concerns constantly racing through their heads (i.e. is the salad dressing fresh, are the steaks cut right, are all shifts staffed, and how many people can be expected today). It is mind boggling, but they show up every day ready to serve their guests, adapting a pleasant and upbeat attitude, and demonstrating their knowledge about food, drink, and service. Are there exceptions? Of course, but in my travels I recognized a positive pattern of commitment in those people that I met.

I was also impressed by the creativity and enthusiasm of some of the chefs. One young man said that it took him two years of testing and mixing various ingredients in order to perfect his Chicken Cordon Bleu. And I found that many chefs take great pride in their homemade sauces, pasta, cakes, pies, and more.

Note that in each entry I included web site addresses, if available, or references to Facebook listings, if applicable. If a restaurant does not have a web site, there are a number of general travel web sites that give the basic information about most restaurants, i.e. address, phone number, specialties and even a map. A few of these general sites are urbanspoon, mytravelguide.com, tripadvisor.com/restaurant, localyahoo.com, menupix.com, diningguide.com, restaurantica.com, superpages.com, travelyahoo.com, and menuism.com.

Also, I have capitalized references to specific dishes that appear in the menu for ease in identifying those same dishes, but general category references such as soups, sandwiches, and desserts are lower case. Also the pricing designation indicates the average price of an entree: $ (inexpensive -up to $10); $$ (mid-price range - $10-20); $$$ (expensive - $21-up), but in almost all restaurants, there are selections that fall in the lower price range.

In some small way, I hoped to not only enlighten visitors as to what Ohio has to offer from a culinary perspective, but also give our local economy a boost by supporting these restaurants with well earned recommendations.

This has been an exciting trip, pun intended, around Ohio and one of discovery: meeting people, exploring some of the more remote towns and villages, and sampling unusual foods. I've enjoyed it all. However, I am not about to hang up my appetite before I write the next book which will feature the recipes of the restaurants featured in *Eating Your Way Across Ohio*. So look for it at your bookstore or online very soon. I will be on the road again!

Happy Travels and Bon Appetit!

Foreword

You are in for a treat! I'm not saying this book will change your life, but it could be a bit life altering, and it just might even get better.

I've heard that the most often asked question is "where are we going to eat tonight?" Well, now Karen Patterson has taken all of the guess work out of it with this book, *Eating Your Way Across Ohio*.

I met Karen some time back at a Book Festival in Kentucky. We sat next to each other signing and selling books. One of my books just happened to be *Eating Your Way Across Kentucky*. I think she was somewhat amazed at the hundreds of people who either bought my book or commented on how much they enjoyed the one they had purchased earlier.

"I want to talk to you about your book," she said. And we did.

The detail and precision she applied in verifying the validity for an eatery's inclusion in this book says a lot about the variety of must places to eat in Ohio.

A five star restaurant here and there is a given, but it's those down home, mom and pops, where the locals eat that have emerged in these pages that can give you that life altering dining experience I mentioned earlier.

For the most part don't expect this to be a gourmet candlelight dining guide. It's not. But it is a list of places to eat good food at reasonable prices in down home surroundings. I can tell you there are restaurants you would never go in until you read about them here.

Eating Your Way Across Ohio will most certainly appeal to Kentuckians alike just like I hope my Kentucky book appeals to those travelers in the Buckeye state.

Here's a suggestion. Turn your book into a traveling diary. When you visit a restaurant, date it, note what you ate and include the receipt. The high quality of this book lends itself to something to be passed down to the kids or grandkids.

There's no excuse. So get up, get out, and get going!

Gary P. West
Author

Acknowledgments

Many people make up the team that accomplishes a project of this magnitude. And many that are deserving of my gratitude for their support, encouragement and help especially as the deadline approached and I was on the road.

My trustworthy assistant, Jolinda Van Dyke, whose charming personality and dedication to this assignment enabled me to visit more than 160 establishments in six months. She organized each visit so that when I arrived at my destination she had already made the contact and briefed the owner or manager about the project so they graciously welcomed me. As one of the most competent and organized people I know, I'm sure I would have been lost at times without her.

Karen Raybould was my travelling partner on a number of occasions despite the personal challenges that she was facing. With years of experience in dealing with the public as a seasoned professional in broadcasting, she was truly an asset and immediately put our hosts at ease during our visits.

I especially want to thank Dr. Nancy Myers for the many hours that she worked with me in sorting through more than 2000 photographs determining which was the right shot that best represented each establishment. Her expertise is remarkable with picture software and I so appreciated help especially considering her busy schedule.

My husband John has not only been both a supporter and an encourager, but the solid foundation that I can always rely on. I am grateful that he respects and understands that the life of a writer is rather isolated since every day brings with it a new deadline. All too often I'm facing my computer monitor and not his sweet smiling face, and this project was no exception. He was patient as I spent countless days on the road though on occasion he joined me. More often than not, however, he was having dinner alone as I enjoyed the exquisite cuisine of another fine restaurant. Despite it all, on more than one occasion I was homesick!

Both my sons, Jesse and Josh Paschke, along with their significant others, Tasia and Leigh, offered their suggestions as to their favorite restaurants especially since their tastes differ from mine. When I followed up on their recommendations, I was always pleasantly surprised since I may have passed up a few of these places.

A friend Chris Wilson was also a great help as he had made many contacts through his business travels in Ohio, and provided me with a number of terrific referrals that I probably would not have found on my own.

I also want to thank Gary West for steering me in the direction of Acclaim Press and for his encouragement in writing this book. He is a busy and prolific writer and I am honored that he wrote the Foreword. And the fine people at Acclaim have been terrific to work with.

So many of the restaurant owners and managers were gracious enough to spend time with me sharing the history and background of their establishments, even though they were often quite busy, and providing me with samples of their signature dishes. Without their cooperation I would not have had the pleasure of writing this book and sharing their specialties with you, the reader.

And, finally, thanks to all of the Chambers and Visitors Bureaus for their suggestions and the vast amount of information they supplied to me about restaurants in their communities.

Eating Your Way Across OHIO

101 MUST PLACES to EAT

NORTH WEST
REGION

Azul Tequila	Napoleon, OH
Briarfield Café	Maumee, OH
The Cabbage Patch Restaurant	Defiance, OH
Dock's Beach House	Port Clinton, OH
The Greek Garden	Findley, OH
Happy Daz	Lima, OH
KemoSabes Roadhouse Grill	Fostoria, OH
Kermit's	Bowling Green, OH
Lamplight Café & Bakery	Perrysburg, OH
Le Petit Gourmet	Maumee, OH
The Orchard Tree	Van Wert, OH
Red Pig Inn	Ottowa, OH
Sullivans Restaurant	Wauseon, OH
The Warehouse Italian Dinners	Marion, OH
Welcome Home Family Dining	Bryan, OH
Woody's Restaurant	Upper Sandusky, OH

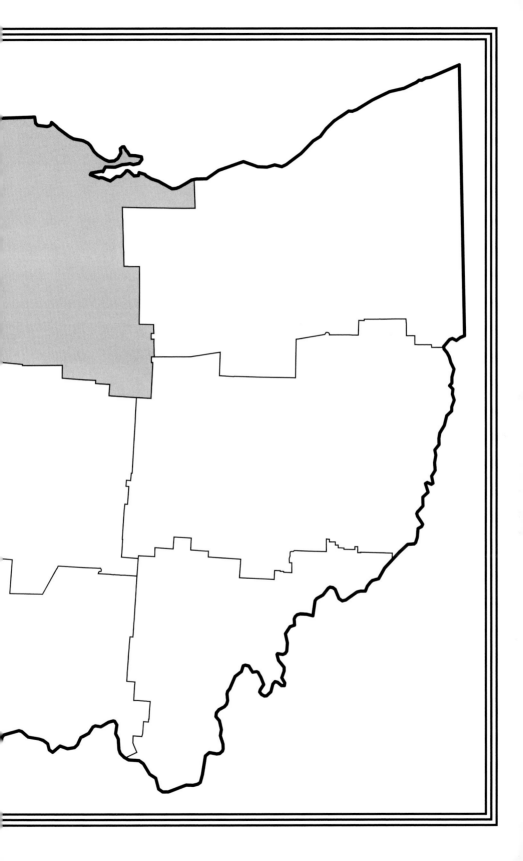

Azul Tequila

Napoleon, OH

Many Mexican restaurants claim they serve authentic Mexican food and for the untraveled American they would probably not know the difference. But Azul Tequila (translated as Blue Tequila) uses recipes that have been passed down through the family for many generations. These recipes have inspired owner Emmanuel Ramirez to provide the very best home-made dishes (the same as those he ate as a child) to his guests with the freshest ingredients.

The entrees are very generous and most are accompanied with beans and Spanish rice. Just a few of the delicious items on the menu include the Pollo Supremo (strips of chicken breast topped with red Mexican sauce and a white cheese sauce), Molcajete Azul (grilled chicken, steak or shrimp covered with green bell peppers, onions, mushrooms and cheese with a green tomatillo and the house molcajete sauce), Arroz Veracruzano (grilled jumbo shrimp on top of rice covered in a white cheese sauce), the Arandenos Steak (16 oz. T-bone topped with grilled shrimp) and the Marimba Steak (pieces of marinated steak with chunks of skewered shrimp). Stuffed burritos, fajitas, tacos and tortillas with a variety of ingredients are also available, as are nachos topped with shrimp, ground beef, beans, chicken or steak and cheese. You definitely won't go away hungry.

Mexican cuisine happens to be my favorite, and while travelling through Mexico and Central America I had the opportunity to sample many authentic dishes from the best kitchens. So I feel pretty confident that what Azul Tequila serves is the real thing.

The service was efficient and our waiter was very attentive, though the language barrier prevents any

small talk beyond giving a basic order from the menu. Emmanuel, on the other hand, speaks almost perfect English and converses quite well.

When you arrive at the building, note the star that Emmanuel has hung to honor his hometown of Arandas, where he departed at the age of thirteen to move to the United States. And while he has been here he has created a pristine establishment with beautiful hand-carved wood chairs and tables. Creative artwork depicting scenes from the Mexican hills and villages grace the expansive walls, and I'm sure these remind him of home. Visiting Azul Tequila is like a culinary excursion to Mexico. Try it, you'll like it!

DINERS INFORMATION

Address
601 E. Riverview Ave., Napoleon, OH 43545
www.azul-tequila.com

Phone
(419) 559-9028

Hours
Monday - Thursday, 11:00 a.m. – 9:30 p.m.
Friday - Saturday, 11:00 a.m. – 10:00 p.m.
Sunday, 11:00 a.m. – 9:00 p.m.

Price Range
$$

Briarfield Café

Maumee, OH

Located in the corner of a small strip mall along Briarfield Blvd., this darling place is a real find. It is neat and clean, and beautifully decorated with a calm blue color scheme and plenty of fascinating knickknacks. Blue happens to be my favorite color and the one I have chosen for my kitchen, so I felt right at home. We met the owners, Jude and Dave Katafiasz, who were charming and shared with us the many challenges they have faced since opening the restaurant in 2004. Many of these ordeals, such as construction on Briarfield Blvd. which resulted in road closings, are out of their control but affect them and the other businesses in the area. Despite it all, they have won the Restaurant of the Year Award and have maintained the business by sticking with their mission, which is to serve all home made dishes with fresh locally purchased ingredients. In fact, Dave said, "If I don't want to eat it, I won't serve it."

We had a chance to sample quite a few of their specialties, which included three types of French Toast (cinnamon swirl, banana bread topped with slices of banana and pecans, and Pecan Caramel – all were unique and quite tasty). We also had the Breakfast Pizza, which is hash browns topped with a cheese omelette, moz-zarella cheese, with salsa and sour cream on the side. Wow! I had never tasted anything like it before and it was simply outstanding.

Breakfast is served all day

and features hand-cut potatoes and homemade bread. One of their most popular items is the Briarfield Salad, which is chocked full of onion, tomatoes, mushrooms, raisins, and topped with Swiss, Feta and Parmesan cheese and served with homemade poppy seed dressing. Like everything else, this was delicious.

Jude and Dave are dedicated to each other and have created a café that is sure to please the hungry, all day and throughout the evening.

DINERS INFORMATION

Address
3220 Briarfield Blvd., Maumee, OH 43537
www.briarfieldcafe.com

Phone
(419) 865-7260

Hours
Monday - Thursday, 7:00 a.m. – 8:00 p.m.
Friday - Saturday, 7:00 a.m. – 9:00 p.m.
Sunday, 7:00 a.m. – 3:00 p.m.

Price Range
$

The Cabbage Patch Restaurant

This is a handy little place though it is off the beaten track and in a remote location of Defiance County. Located near the Auglaize River, it is just a stone's throw away from the area where families fish, boat or swim.

The Cabbage Patch not only serves as a carry-out where all the necessary items like soda, snacks, ice cream, toilet tissue, canned food and beer can be purchased, but comfort food is also available. Nothing fancy, but a satisfying selection that will fill the void whether you are just passing through or spending the day by the river. It's also convenient so you don't have to fire up the grill. Weather permitting, you can eat outside where there is a scenic view and the sound of the water soothes away the cares of the day.

The menu offers a variety of subs, pizzas, and wings along with a selection of sandwiches.

Subs are served either hot or cold and include the Smothered Chicken with green peppers, mushrooms and a choice of cheese on a hardy bun. The Philly Beef Sub, which features slices of tender steak topped with onions, peppers and melted cheese, is the deluxe version of the Steak and Cheese Sub. The Chicken Bacon Ranch is just as it sounds but with a layer of cheese. And the Southwest Chicken Sub is filled with chicken, peppers (jalapenos or green), tomatoes, and a rich southwestern sauce that combines the robust flavors of salsa and ranch dressing.

Pizzas are available in three sizes: the 16-inch that can feed a family of six; the 12-inch that serves a group of four; or the

personal pizza that is perfect for just one. Of course, these portions depend on how hungry the crowd is. A few of the Cabbage Patch specialties are the Meat Lovers that is loaded with pepperoni and sausage along with a choice of toppings. The Hawaiian that is laced with chunks of pineapple sunk deep in tomato sauce and topped with melted cheese. Or the Barbeque Chicken with a spicy tangy taste. And for that gourmet pizza lover, there are specials that feature a creamy white sauce instead of a tomato base. The Philly Beef Steak, Chicken Bacon Ranch and the Spinach Chicken Alfredo all add a new twist to the old time favorite pizza.

And don't forget about the wings. There are tender breaded wings as well as the boneless Chicken Chunk Basket, and both are served with a choice of sauces.

Whether you eat in or take out, you can pick up a few groceries at the same time. Also, as an added note, at press time the owners Kathy and Pete Schlegel were planning to build a gas station adjacent to the carry-out to provide additional services to the community.

Address
19492 St. Rt. 637, Defiance, OH 43512
Phone
(419) 393-2271
Hours
Daily, 7:00 a.m. – 10:00 p.m.
Price Range
$

Dock's Beach House

Port Clinton, OH

Dock's is located on the north shore of Lake Erie. Nearby are Port Clinton, Catawba Island, the Lake Erie Islands including Put-in Bay, so it is centrally located and not far from the main activity in the area. This fun and festive family oriented restaurant overlooks the water, and the lake breezes constantly blow into shore where the panoramic view is outstanding. In the distance, I could see the islands as I stood on the 500 foot sandy beach adjacent to Dock's where you can swim, enjoy a meal or just simply relax with a good book.

I came upon Dock's at just the right time because they had recently opened their newly renovated restaurant. Pictures of the before version depict a totally different place, and some of the patrons said that the new addition with a spacious deck and expanded air conditioned indoor eating area does not compare to the way it used to be. They said it is so much better and much more fun.

Dock's is seasonal and only open from May 1 to October 31, when most of the action in the area ceases for the winter. During the off-season, owner Ed Fitzgerald is able to make repairs and even renovate the business as he did in 2011. He also heads to Florida to handle his varied business ventures while his capable manager, Debbie Hirt, handles the day-to-day operations, but also takes time off during the winter months.

As a beach resort, it is only natural that Dock's specialty is fresh fish and seafood. Entrees such as Peel & Eat Shrimp, sautéed Prince Edward Island Mussels, Broiled Walleye, Deep Fried Lake Erie Perch and Alaskan King Crab are sure to please those inlanders that have travelled to the sunny shores for a little R & R. The North Atlantic Salmon and Tilapia are also very popular and are served grilled, pan seared or blackened.

Not to ignore the red meat eaters in the crowd, Dock's offers the New York Strip or Choice Top Sirloin Steaks, which are char-grilled to order and served with three sides. Two desserts are always on the menu and vary from day to day, but who can pass up the likes of Vanilla Bean Cheesecake and Chocolate Raspberry Volcano Cake.

Unadvertised specials for lunch and dinner are offered daily and are the result of the creative chefs, Made (emphasis on the "e") and Chuck, so ask the server what these two have cooked up on any given day.

The mellow sound of live music playing in the background while the sound of waves lapping on the beach will sooth even the most restless soul. Whether you have a whopping appetite or just want to eat light; whether you are still on stress time or have fallen in with the beat of lake time, Dock's provides good food and a great atmosphere to let your hair down and un-wind.

DINERS INFORMATION

Address
252 W. Lakeshore Dr., Port Clinton, OH 43452
www.docksbeachhouse.com

Phone
(419) 732-6609

Hours
Sunday - Thursday, 11:00 a.m. – Midnight
Friday - Saturday, 11:00 a.m. – 2:30 p.m.

Price Range
$$$

23

The Greek Garden

Findley, OH

After years of working in construction and with his first son due to enter the world, Beau Thompson decided to change careers and buy the Greek restaurant that had occupied the 1890s building and operated in downtown Findlay for more than 25 years before closing. After little more than two weeks to totally revamp the place, The Greek Garden was reopened. As the only Greek restaurant in Findlay, Thompson has made his mark by using the freshest, locally purchased ingredients that are prepared for each shift while he oversees each dish that is served. He even takes a turn at cooking and really shows his hand when he prepares his signature Sizzling Flat Iron Steak, which is an 8 ounce certified Angus beef steak topped with his special sauce and onion.

The décor is laced with plenty of grape vines and words of wisdom from the Greek gods. Tables are covered with custom made muted rainbow cloths covered with thick glass that is so clean it was almost invisible. His attention to detail is obvious, from the dining and banquet rooms to the kitchen and even restrooms. Everything is spotless and inviting.

In addition to Friday night's special of roasted lamb shanks with Mediterranean potatoes, Thompson features daily specials along with his popular dishes of Spanakopita (spinach pie with feta and parmesan cheeses layered with buttery phyllo dough), Gyros (pronounced euros), and Saganaki (cheese lit on fire at the table and served with warm home-

made seasoned pita chips). The Greek Garden Hummus (Mediterranean bean dip and signature spices) is the best I've tasted since visiting Israel. Salads come in two sizes, but both are very large with a generous variety of fresh veggies. You definitely get your money's worth and will most likely be taking home a doggie bag.

This is a family place where the kids' all-you-can-eat menu not only offers a Greek plate of Gyro meat, pita and veggies, but also Mini Corn Dogs, Chicken Fries, and Grilled Cheese.

Beer and wine are available, along with Thompson's specialty drink Sangria prepared to order.

His plans for an outdoor dining area should be completed by the time this book is released. Overall, this is truly a tasty experience.

DINERS INFORMATION

Address
321 S. Main St., Findley, OH 45840
www.thegreekgarden.com

Phone
(419) 422-0808

Hours
Monday - Thursday, 11:00 a.m. – 8:00 p.m.
Friday - Saturday, 11:00 a.m. – 9:00 p.m.
Closed Sunday

Price Range
$$

Happy Daz

Lima, OH

This carry out or eat in restaurant is a take off of the television show by the same name, but different spelling. The 1950s theme depicts an era when life was simpler and easier than in current times, and this attitude is reflected on the menu. Old-time favorites like Banana Splits, Peanut Butter Parfaits, Strawberry Shortcake, sundaes, shakes, cones and malts are not only popular because of their simplicity, but because they are doggone good. All are specialty items one would see served on the original Happy Days show. But in addition to desserts, Happy Daz serves some pretty hardy food, too. Burgers and sandwiches, Loaded Mashed Potato Bowls and Diner Classics like Breaded or Grilled Pork Tenderloin, Texas Grilled Cheese, the classic BLT and an All-Beef Footlong Coney. There is also Tuna and Chicken Salad, but they also sell plenty of the old stand-by, Mac and Cheese. Rich, cheesy and creamy, this was the best I have ever had and I can understand why they sell so much if it.

Owner John Heaphy got his start in the food sales business early in life when he was selling sandwiches from his shoulder strap box on a number of construction sites in Lima. By 17, he was selling sandwiches at the county fair, which allowed him to earn enough money to buy his first restaurant. He would eventually own many restaurants before he settled on Happy Daz.

This place is nothing fancy, but the food is good and the price is right.

DINERS INFORMATION

Address
1064 Bellefontaine Ave., Lima, OH 45804

Phone
(419) 227-3663

Hours
Monday - Saturday, 7:00 a.m. – 10:00 p.m.
Sunday, 8:00 a.m. – 10:00 p.m.

Price Range
$

KemoSabes Roadhouse Grill

Fostoria, OH

S ituated on the edge of Fostoria, this spot is popular with the local community and was quite busy when I arrived. It truly is a roadhouse, with rustic barn siding on the interior walls and an old fashioned bar that reminded me of those I have seen in many western movies. As is typical in most restaurants, there are televisions in the bar area. Antique bikes and farm tools adorn the walls and there is plenty of space to stretch out.

The food is down home good and fills the empty spot in one's stomach. The appetizers include the Roadhouse Nachos, El Paso Pickles, which are hand breaded, fried and served with Sabe sauce, but the Kemosabe Flatbread is the best. The fresh white dough is loaded with roasted garlic and fresh arugula and topped with three cheeses – gorgonzola, feta and parmesan. In addition to salads, there is a selection of soups – Sweet Corn Chowder, Ham and Cabbage and "Don't Mess with Texas" Chilli.

Of course, no Texas-style roadhouse would be complete without a fine selection of meat, and there are a variety of steaks to choose from - the 8 oz. Sheriff's Strip Steak, the Dude Ranch Ribeye, the Tenderloin Express and the Lone Ranger, a full pound of sirloin that is flame grilled to perfection. All are 100% certified Angus beef and are served with a healthy portion of roasted garlic, herb butter, salad and sides.

Also featured are a number of burgers including a Buffalo Bleu Burger grilled to order with creamy blue cheese and delicate, crispy onion strings on the side. If you are into pasta, you won't be disappointed with the Basil Garlic Fettucini, Ancho Chicken Penne or the Border Bolognese, which is a combination of spiced Italian sausage and ground beef in a marinara sauce tossed with rigatoni pasta.

What caught my eye was the Rustic Chicken Noodle Mash. A hearty chicken soup, which is my favorite, complete with chunks of carrots and onions, delicate seasonings, and served over mashed, garlic redskin potatoes, another one of my favorites. Both combined makes a perfect meal for my taste.

An excellent meal should be complimented by an excellent dessert, and any on the dessert menu would hit the spot. Either the Deep Dish Cookie or Ice Cream Fun Day sundae would be satisfying. And the New York Style Cheesecake or simply an ice cream float would do very well, too.

As their slogan says, "Where Friends Gather," so bring your friends and enjoy a gathering with this delicious comfort food.

DINERS INFORMATION

Address
820 Sandusky St., Fostoria, OH 44830
www.kemosabes.com

Phone
(419) 435-3000

Hours
Tuesday - Thursday, 11:00 a.m. – 9:00 p.m.
Friday - Saturday, 11:00 a.m. – 9:00 p.m.
Closed Monday

Price Range
$$

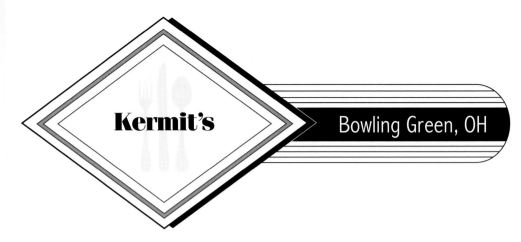

Kermit's

Bowling Green, OH

Family owned since 1986, Jim Maas and his daughter Cassy, along with other family members, run the day-to-day operations at Kermit's. Located in the heart of downtown Bowling Green just blocks from Bowling Green State University, Kermit's is a great place to catch a reasonably priced meal. It is a pillar of the community and has served thousands of students and their families over the years. At the same time it has a casual and comfortable atmosphere where, as the saying goes, "everyone knows your name," or just about. Everyone is welcome whether you are a regular or a first time guest. The décor is highlighted with family pictures and the farm tools of Kermit Lambert, the namesake of the restaurant.

Breakfast is served all day for those students who start their day late and features the usual – eggs, toast, hot cakes, biscuits and gravy, bacon and ham with a few variations. As an added bonus, steak, chipped beef or corned beef hash can be included with egg dishes. And many items are available à la carte. Of course, hot coffee and tea are always available for a pick me up at any time.

Lunch and dinner are served all day too and feature Chili Cheese Fries, Hot Roast Beef and Roast Turkey, Fish-N-Chips, Spaghetti, Grilled Catfish, Fried Shrimp and Shrimp Basket, BBQ Ribs, Beef and Noodles, and Scalloped Potatoes and Ham. There is also a wide choice of chicken dishes prepared in a variety of ways, including Boneless Wings, Drummies, Grilled Breast, Honey Fried and Breast Patties. And the "Pick 3 Build a Platter" is a great way of customizing an order to suite any taste. In other words, pick a sandwich – Kermit Melt, Turkey Bacon Melt, Turkey Club, Philly Cheese Steak, Rueben – and add a couple of sides. Voilà! A meal that is sure to please. On the lighter side, salads are generous and prepared with all fresh ingredients.

Kermit's specialty is the Tandoories, which is named for the Tandoori Naan flatbread, is hand made in Tandoori clay ovens. Traditionally, food cooked in this manner is exposed to direct fire and very high temperatures approaching 900° F, and is often used in Middle Eastern cooking. The Tandoori bread served at Kermit's is purchased already prepared and packaged. Then it is grilled until crispy on the outside and chewy on the inside and stuffed with a choice of items, like Bacon, Lettuce and Tomato (BLT), Grilled or Greek Chicken, Taco ingredients, all topped with a savory or sweet sauce prepared in house. According to Cassy, this is an all time favorite and they have made hundreds of Tandoories since they introduced it on their menu.

Jim is also proud of their homemade desserts: fruit and cream pies, New York style Cheesecake and especially the Hot Fudge Cake. No out of the box mixes here; only the best for Kermit's guests.

Though there are many restaurants that line the streets of this college town, Kermit's is one of a kind, where homemade food is savored and families can feel that it is their home away from home.

Lamplight Café & Bakery

About 25 years ago, Deanna Montion's father, James Haas, started a little bakery business in Perrysburg. Deanna spent quite a bit of time there and when she was old enough her father, who was nearing retirement age, asked if she would take over the helm of the business. Hesitantly, she agreed. Even though she was a baker, she did it for pleasure and on a much smaller scale than what was required at the store. It was only after she took over that she realized how he had built up the business not only as a bakery, but also as a café where breakfast and lunch are served all day.

The first aroma I smelled as I walked through the door had me hooked and my taste buds went into overdrive. One look at the display case with all of the scrumptious cookies and huge round muffins also had me and a little voice inside my head said, "Feed me, Seymour!" But the decision was difficult. Selecting a cookie from the wide variety that Deanna makes is nearly impossible. There are chocolate chip, peanut butter, oatmeal raisin, lemon and orange drop, frosted sugar and chocolate chocolate (that's not a typo. It is a double chocolate cookie.). Other special varieties of cut out cookies are available during the year, like apple cookies during September, pumpkin cookies during October, and Christmas trees, stars and bells during the holidays. And then there are the muffins: blueberry, cappuccino

chunk, cherry cheesecake, butter rum, orange, apple strudel and cinnamon twist. Like the cookies, the muffins also vary throughout the year.

All the bakery items are made in the modest kitchen at the store, mainly by Deanna. But if guests are not interested in a sweet treat, they can have a sandwich (chicken salad, Reuben and grilled bologna are most popular) on freshly baked bread or soup made fresh daily.

Deanna has done a fine job of upholding her end of the deal with her father, and has created a lovely place with tablecloth covered tables and hanging vines and flowers. It's a great place to drop by for lunch, or at least a cookie.

DINERS INFORMATION

Address
121 W. Indiana Ave., Perrysburg, OH 43551
Check them out on Facebook

Phone
(419) 874-0125

Hours
Monday - Friday, 7:00 a.m. – 2:30 p.m.
Saturday, 7:00 a.m. – 2:00 p.m.
Closed Sunday

Price Range
$

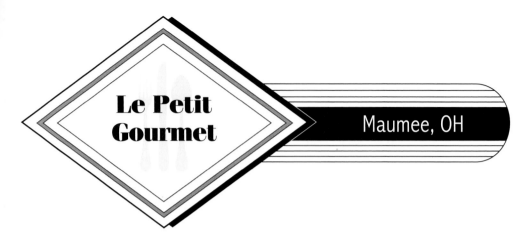

Le Petit Gourmet

Maumee, OH

Conveniently located in the center of a busy industrial park, Le Petit Gourmet caters to its neighbors literally and figuratively. It provides catering for special events to area businesses, but it caters to the needs of walk-ins that are looking for a sandwich, salad and a cold drink in a relaxing atmosphere where they can unwind. The part of the business that I was concerned with, however, was what this deli had to offer the average person off the street. The display cases were stacked with cold cuts, cheeses and salad items, while the chef at the grill was busy cooking up Reubens, Cheesy Philly Steaks and Chicken Fajitas. The salads are not the common every day variety but feature Seafood Supreme, Rotini Pasta, Tortellini, Broccoli, Waldorf, Chicken and Tuna salad. All sounded yummy.

And the bakery offers Filled Croissants with chocolate, strawberry, and cream cheese, as well as cinnamon and butter croissants. In addition, there is a variety of pastries, such as strudels and Danish, along with cheesecake and carrot cake.

Not only can you have your lunch promptly prepared to go or delivered to your location, but their comfortable dining area allows you to read the paper, watch the latest news or sports, meet with a friend, and at the same time have a well-balanced and healthy meal. Sit at the counter or in one of the large booths.

Whether you are travelling thorough the area or you work here, Le Petit can provide an excellent quick meal at a reasonable price.

Address
6546 Weatherfield Ct., Maumee, OH 43537
Phone
(419) 866-6343
Hours
Monday - Saturday, 7:30 a.m. – 5:30 p.m.
Closed for scheduled events on Sunday
Price Range
$

The Orchard Tree

Van Wert, OH

This large diner-type restaurant is located outside of town on the main street, so it's easy to find especially if you look for their trademark orchard tree on the sign. Once inside, the dining area is spacious and decorated with many large framed pictures of area high school sports teams, which I'm sure thrills the kids when they come in after games. Other than that, the place is nondescript. There are windows around the entire building so there's plenty of light, and the long buffet table is set up on one side of the dining area.

I spoke to Angie, who told me about the breakfast buffet on the weekends and the daily dinner buffet. There is also a daily Soup and Salad Bar that includes hot items like soup and a variety of other hot items. The Deluxe Soup and Salad Bar includes the soup and cold items only, but nothing from the hot side. In addition to the buffet, there are daily specials throughout the week that include homemade Meatloaf, a Chicken or Tuna Salad Sandwich, Beef Noodles over mashed potatoes, Polish Sausage and Kraut, Swiss Mushroom Burger, Swiss steak with dressing and mashed potatoes, or a Salmon Patty, to name only a few choices.

The menu also features an extensive breakfast list and even an à la carte section (i.e. English muffin, oatmeal, corn beef hash, bagel and cream cheese), which is perfect for ordering just a small meal at a very reasonably priced. Orchard Tree is an excellent breakfast place. However, there are a few of the more popular dishes on the dinner side that includes the Harvest Fried Chicken, the 8 ounce Delmonico Steak and the 10 ounce New York Strip Steak. A special Seniors' menu also offers dishes at a special price.

Whatever you choose, you won't be disappointed because the food is good, the place is clean, and the service is quick unless you eat from the buffet and then it is at your own pace. And they support the community.

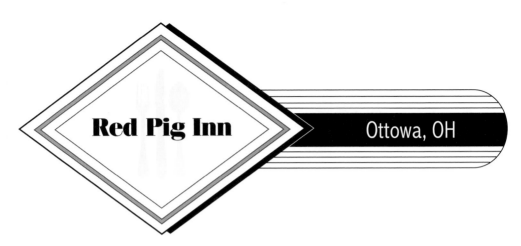

Red Pig Inn

Ottowa, OH

Established in 1975, the Red Pig Inn was the brainchild of Richard and Paulette Schnipke, who worked long hours to become established as the premier barbeque place in Ottowa and beyond. As the main cook and manager, Richard cooked in primitive conditions at first with very few conveniences in his kitchen, but somehow he managed. Gradually, the restaurant was expanded to include five dining rooms with space for large groups and banquets. The décor has a down home comfy feeling with wooden tables and checkered table clothes, and displays of the pig mascot are in many of the nooks crannies in the restaurant.

The name originated with the idea that the main specialty of the restaurant would be barbeque pork sandwiches, ribs and chops. The place caught on because of its name recognition, but also became popular as a great place to get BBQ.

The Red Pig Inn has been awarded numerous local, state and national awards that include the Ohio Pork Restaurant of the Year, the Top 12 Pork Restaurants in the USA, Ohio State Fair Rib Cook Off winner, Northwest Ohio Rib Cook Off People's Choice winner, the Lima News Readers' Survey for Best Ribs, and the Most Creative Menu. Many of these awards have been received a number of times, which was quite evident when we entered the front lobby where numerous awards and trophies were displayed. It looked like a trophy store. Instead, we were awestruck by the recognition and the

accolades this one restaurant has received, so we anticipated a good meal and were not disappointed.

We had Porky's Delight, which is pulled pork drenched in the award winning mild BBQ sauce. The pork was tender and not stringy as it sometimes can be. We also had tender ribs that fell off the bone and could be eaten with just a fork or fingers, but either way they pleased the palate. And the homemade chips were crispy and perfect for dipping in the sauce that has a variety of degrees of spiciness. I found the names for a few of these degrees to be quite entertaining. Of course, there is the regular, mild and hot sauce, but there is also squealer and squealer hot, as well as the Jim Beam sauce.

Whatever your level of squealing might be, make sure you stop by for some mighty fine BBQ.

DINERS INFORMATION

Address
1470 N. Perry St., Ottowa, OH 45875
www.redpiginn.com

Phone
(419) 523-6458

Hours
Monday - Thursday, 11:00 a.m. – 9:30 p.m.
Friday - Saturday, 11:00 a.m. – 11:30 p.m.
Sunday, 11:00 a.m. – 10:00 p.m.

Price Range
$$

Sullivans Restaurant

Wauseon, OH

Sullivans Restaurant came about as a result of an unfortunate event that took place in downtown Waseon, but it has turned out to be most beneficial to the community. A large fire consumed almost the entire block where Sullivans now stands and took with it all the buildings that were located there. After the ruins were finally cleared away, this restaurant was built with the cooperation of almost the entire town and rose like the Phoenix from the ashes. Impressed by the support they received, owners Scott Sullivan and Brian Roth resolved that this effort would "write a new chapter in the history of our community. And when you do, you might just forget you're sitting at the corner of Fulton and Elm."

Once I entered the glass doors of this attractive brick building, I understood the meaning of their mission statement. I certainly did not feel that I was sitting in a small sleepy town in northwest Ohio, but more like an upscale metropolitan eatery in Chicago or L.A. The décor is precise and crisp, with attractive contemporary artwork displayed throughout the dining and bar areas. And on the entrance wall there is an exhibit of full color photographs of area landmarks. The mission statement reflects the fortitude of the town's people in building this fine restaurant: "Our décor reflects on the history of those who came before us and is a reminder of the possibilities the future holds."

The menu also reflects a cosmopolitan focus with signature entrees that include Balsamic Chicken, Grilled Salmon with Herb Lemon Butter Sauce, Creamy Cajun Pasta, Rigatoni Bolognese and Filet Steak Medallions. Chicken, pasta, seafood and steak dishes have been designed to please every palate.

Burgers, from quarter to half pound, are offered in a variety of

ways – with a choice of cheese as well as jalapenos and Cajun style. And on the lighter side the choices of wraps, soups, salads and sandwiches are abundant.

This is more than a dining experience, it is an inspiration as to how a small town can pull together to overcome adversity and succeed. Their statement: "We make it all… better," says it all.

DINERS INFORMATION

Address
141 Fulton St., Wauseon, OH 43567
www.sullivanswauseon.com

Phone
(419) 335-0790

Hours
Monday - Thursday, 11:00 a.m. – 11:00 p.m.
Friday - Saturday, 11:00 a.m. – 1:00 a.m.
Closed Sunday

Price Range
$$

The Warehouse Italian Dinners

Marion, OH

Don't let the name fool you! The Warehouse is open for both lunch and dinner. When asked about their specialty, manager Michelle Knapp said they have great sun dried tomato pesto and the best Chicken and Mushroom Alfredo around. She was right on both counts. The tomato pesto is rich and thick with a hint of Italian spices served over a tender rigatoni pasta and perfect to soak up with the flaky crusty homemade Italian bread. The Mushroom Alfredo is thick and creamy with a combination of delicate seasonings.

Though ordering from the menu is available, a lunch buffet features a variety of salads, pastas and sauces, along with homemade desserts (fruit cobblers and brownies), all made from scratch. The feature soup of the day when I visited was Cream of Potato, which was full of flavor with bite-sized chunks of potatoes, slivers of carrots and a hint of garlic.

Not only is the food an excursion in Italian cuisine, but the building itself, situated in downtown Marion, is quite impressive. Constructed in 1925 and known as the CDM, it originally housed the Inter Urban, which was the electric train that ran from Marion to Delaware and then on to Columbus. In 1994, the massive building was converted into a restaurant and, to date, only half of it is actually used for dining. Influenced by the 1940s and 50s, the theme

has been captured in the music of Frank Sinatra, Louis Armstrong, and Glenn Miller playing in the background, while discretely positioned televisions in the main dining room play movies featuring Roy Rogers and Dale Evans, John Wayne, and Gary Cooper. Bookshelves are bursting with period knick knacks, classic liquor bottles, trophies and toys. Nearby are the old-fashioned Coke machines that delivered this popular drink in glass bottles. And on the wall hangs a huge clown face that I can only imagine was displayed in a penny arcade at one time.

This is a great place to eat, especially after taking in a show at the nearby Marion Palace Theater. And when you visit, ask for either Michelle or assistant manager Kyle Reinwald who will give you the history of the building and will just treat you right! As their slogan says, this is truly "A Reunion of Food and Family."

Address
320 W. Center St., Marion, OH 43302
www.thewarehouseitalian.com
Phone
(740) 387-8124
Hours
Monday - Friday, 11:00 a.m. – 3:00 p.m. (lunch)
Monday - Thursday, 5:00 p.m. – 9:00 p.m. (dinner)
Friday - Saturday, 5:00 p.m. – 10:00 p.m.
Price Range
$$

Welcome Home Family Dining

Bryan, OH

At one time years ago, the Bryan newsstand was housed at the site of the Welcome Home Diner where it stood until a new restaurant came into town. Eventually, Terry Rumel purchased the building and replaced the newsstand with the restaurant. It was not long before the Welcome Home Diner was "born" and people looked to it as a home away from home where they could eat down home cooking.

Today the chicken served in the diner is farm fresh and raised locally. Everything, including the soups, potatoes and desserts, are homemade by Betty in a small kitchen in the back of the restaurant, where she is able to work miracles. I had the potato soup that was creamy with chunks of potato and chopped onion. It was excellent. And the Chocolate Chocolate (you read that right, it's double chocolate) cake was rich with a thick layer of

chocolate icing that melted in my mouth. I could just feel the extra calories, but it was worth it because it was so delicious. Betty also makes a pretty good Vinegar Cake, which is her specialty and a big hit with the patrons.

This isn't a fancy place and, in fact, there are very few decorations on the walls or even on the counters, but there is plenty of room to sit "for a spell" and there is always Betty's cooking to enjoy and her famous Vinegar Cake.

Address
136 N. Main St., Bryan, OH 43506

Phone
(419) 636-1365

Hours
Monday - Friday, 6:00 a.m. – 4:00 p.m.
Saturday - Sunday, 6:00 a.m. – 2:00 p.m.

Price Range
$

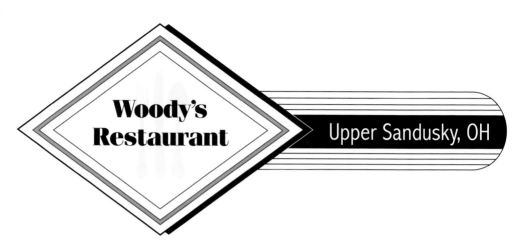

Woody's Restaurant

Upper Sandusky, OH

Woody's is conveniently located at the intersection of U.S. Rt. 23 and St. Rt. 199, and can be easily seen from the highway. Situated half way between Columbus and Toledo going north and south, and Lima and Mansfield going west to east, it is not surrounded by other stores or businesses, but it is worth the stop and has plenty of parking.

Though initially I thought the name Woody's originated with the renowned OSU coach when I saw related memorabilia and souvenirs in the display case in the lobby, owner Chuck Coons clarified that it was named for the original owner of the restaurant.

The Victorian theme is beautifully carried out through the spacious dining room with refinished oak antique dressers and tables along with colorfully fringed Victorian lamps. The oak paneling combined with the delicately flowered blue wallpaper and the burgundy tablecloths provide a comforting atmosphere that gave me the feeling of coming home again. A set of signature plates depicting scenes from the movie *Gone With the Wind* along with a display of delicate antique china plates grace the walls in the entrance way.

The Bow and Arrow Lounge displays a more quaint and rugged theme with a full size canoe hanging from the ceiling. The atmosphere is relaxed especially on Fridays from 4:00-7:00 during Happy Hour when hot appetizers are provided along with favorite beverages.

Specials are offered daily for both lunch and dinner in the dining room as well as a variety of homemade seasonal soups. The Tavern Battered Cod and the Lake Erie Perch are popular and guests drive in from miles around for one of their freshly cut steaks (Porterhouse, New York Strip and Filet Mignon), but the official house specialty is Prime Rib, hand cut and grilled to order.

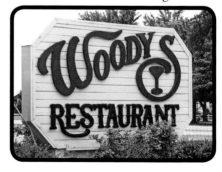

And if you are looking for seafood, there are always two entrees on the menu for dinner.

No meal would be complete without one of Alice Wolf's homemade desserts. She's been making pies at Woody's almost from the time it opened, but she's been perfecting her recipes years before that. She said her husband always had to have dessert after his meal so she created a few specialties of her own which she further refined during her work at the restaurant. And refined she did. The Bread Pudding was delectable! The combination of the firm crusty bread flavored with pecans and creamy vanilla pudding, all topped with a mouthwatering sauce, is heavenly.

This is a great place where the family can relax over a fine meal before continuing their journey.

DINERS INFORMATION

Address
1350 N. Warpole St., Upper Sandusky, OH 43351
www.woodysrestaurant.com

Phone
(419) 294-1434

Hours
Tuesday - Friday, 11:00 a.m. – 2:00 p.m. (lunch); 4:00 p.m. – 9:30 p.m. (dinner)
Saturday, 4:00 p.m. – 9:30 p.m.
Closed Sunday and Monday

Price Range
$$

NORTH EAST
REGION

356 Fighter Group	North Canton, OH
Ashland-Wooster Drive In	Ashland, OH
Best Friends	Mentor, OH
Casa Fiesta	Norwalk, OH
Chowder House Café	Cuyahoga Falls, OH
CW Burgersteins Great Sandwich Works	Wooster, OH
Doc's Deli	Mansfield, OH
Fairport Family Restaurant	Fairport Harbor, OH
Melvin's Brick Oven and Bakery	Wooster, OH
Mohican Tavern	Loudonville, OH
Pickle Bill's on the Waterfront	Grand River, OH
The Pufferbelly Ltd.	Kent, OH
Spats Café	Mentor, OH
TJ's Restaurant	Wooster, OH

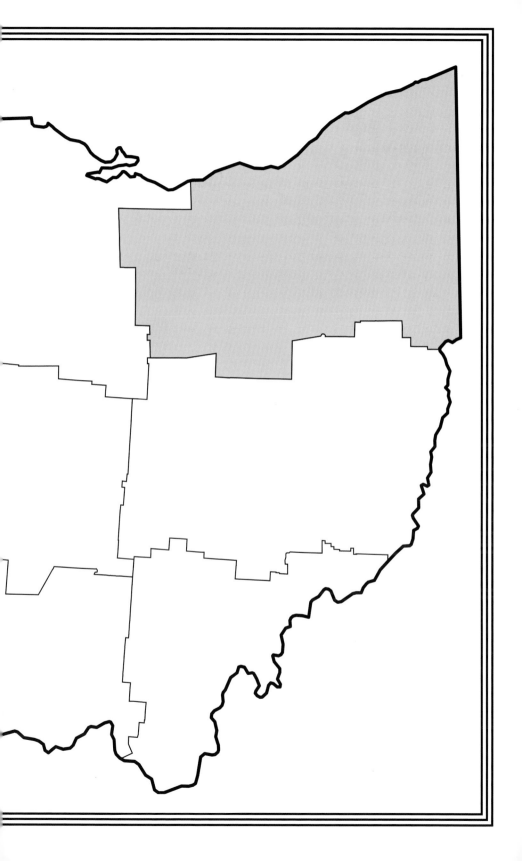

356 Fighter Group

North Canton, OH

"Kilroy was here?" was a common saying during the 1940s, but I feel that he had actually been at the 356 Fighter Group Restaurant, or at least should have been because it is one of three authentic WWII theme restaurants still operating in the country dedicated to our heroes of that war. Having written a memoir (*Allies Forever: The Life and Times of an American Prisoner of War*, 2009, Outskirts Press) about my father's experience as a prisoner of war in WWII, I was looking forward to visiting the 356 Fighter Group. Built in 1986, it overlooks the Akron Canton airport. Outside are genuine military vehicles and the stone building housing the restaurant looks like it has been there since the 1940s.

Once inside, almost every square inch of wall space is filled with fascinating memorabilia, such as placards depicting soldiers, their crews and families, china plates, vintage posters, newspaper articles, and other period items. A

battered wing from a war plane hangs from the ceiling along with a bomb casing. Everywhere I looked there were antiques. Even the two fireplaces are decorated to recreate those found in pre-war homes while Frank Sinatra, Bing Crosby, the Andrew Sisters and songs of the Big Bands play in the background. It certainly is an experience to observe the artifacts of that period in history.

The food is a bit more modern with Prime Rib smothered with onions and mushrooms, Potato Crusted Chicken, Sirloin Kabob, Aunt Edna's Pulled Pork and a variety of burgers with military names, like The Aviator, The General's Ultimate Cheeseburger, The Duke and the Bruiser. Speaking of Kilroy, they have named a meatloaf after him. I had the Wisconsin Cheese Soup that was smooth and cheesy with a touch of Tabasco® that gave it a kick. The Vegetable Quiche that is baked daily was quite tasty, but would have been better with a little ham mixed with the cheese. The Pasta Salad with bowtie pasta and banana sweet pepper was delicious with olive oil and Balsamic vinegar. The Crab Stuffed Shrimp was truly out of his world with the perfect blend of real crab and shrimp. And before I left, owner Bob Scofield gave me a gift of a loaf of homemade bread in a round loaf and a piece of warm apple pie with a cinnamon brown sugar topping. Both were indescribably delicious, and I was totally content as I drove off into the sunset.

Address
4919 Mt. Pleasant Rd., North Canton, OH 44720
www.356fg.com

Phone
(330) 494-3500

Hours
Monday - Saturday, 11:00 a.m. – 4:00 p.m. (dining room)
Friday - Saturday, 4:00 p.m. – 11:00 p.m. (lounge)
Sunday, 10:00 a.m. – 2:00 p.m. (brunch)
Sunday, 4:00 p.m. – 9:00 p.m. (lounge)
Monday - Thurdsay, 4:00 p.m. – 10:00 p.m. (lounge)

Price Range
$$

Ashland-Wooster Drive In

Ashland, OH

I remember drive-in restaurants from my childhood and thought they were as extinct as the dinosaurs, but sure enough there is one left and it is located on the main street going into Ashland from I-70. Actually, I was skeptical that this would be the drive-in of my youth when carhops came out to the car, took the order and delivered it on a neat little tray that attached to the window. But that is exactly what they do at Ashland-Wooster Drive In. In fact, that is the only way you can place an order besides going to the drive through window. There is no inside seating, but there are picnic tables if eating in the car is not quite your style.

I always enjoyed this novel convenience way back when and that has not changed. What I also enjoyed at this drive-in were the menu choices that are limited to hot dogs with a variety of toppings (homemade coney sauce and cole slaw, sauerkraut, chili, hot sauce, cheese and bacon crumbles). There are also sandwiches (shredded chicken, perch, veal, ham, roast beef and all veggie), and side orders that seem to be endless, from fried pickles, mini corn dogs, and mushrooms to shrimp, clams and boneless chicken wings. Wash it all down with homemade root beer, southern sweet tea, a milk shake or the usual commercial soft drinks that can also be made up as a float.

52

Being a hot dog lover, I ordered one with cheese, bacon and chili along with order of fresh cut fries, and an iced mug of root beer. It was like going back in time to the old A & W Root Beer Stands that were the predecessors of fast food restaurants. Upon further investigation, I discovered that this drive-in started out as an A & W back in 1957. It was sold to Joann and Bud Bemiller in 1969, who eventually sold it to their son and daughter-in-law, Steve and Deb Bemiller, who are the current owners. Now their children are in line to work and eventually own the restaurant some day. After more than five decades in the same location and more than four decades in the same family, this dinosaur is thankfully still alive. In a world of fast food restaurants on almost every corner, this was a find that I would not have passed up.

DINERS INFORMATION

Address
1134 E. Main St., Ashland, OH 44805
www.ashland-wooster.com

Phone
(419) 281-2658

Hours
Monday - Thursday, 11:00 a.m. – 9:00 p.m.
Friday - Saturday, 11:00 a.m. – 9:30 p.m.
Sunday, Noon – 9:00 p.m.

Price Range
$

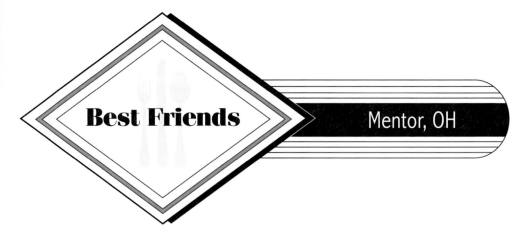

Best Friends

Mentor, OH

"Where Good Friends and Family Eat"

Located only a mile or so from the shores of Lake Erie, I found this to be an excellent breakfast place especially if you want to get an early start to go fishing or swimming. Breakfast is served all day and, in fact, there is an economical Early Bird Favorite where breakfast comes with two eggs, home fries or grits and toast for $3.00. At the other end of the day, there is an Early Bird Dinner Special with six entrees to choose from including Chopped Sirloin, Homemade Meatloaf, Baked Whitefish, Baby Beef Liver, Grilled Ham Steak, and Spaghetti and Meatballs. All are served with a choice of a potato (except the pasta) and vegetables, soup, salad, roll and dessert —

all for one price. Then there is Crazy Kids Night on Tuesday, when kids under 12 can eat FREE from a kid friendly menu. They can take their pick from Grilled Cheese, Hamburger/Cheeseburger, Baked Meatloaf, Chicken Fingers and Fish-n-Chips.

There is also a good selection on the lunch and dinner menus, and I'm sure there is a dish to please every taste.

I had the Mushroom Swiss Omelet that was made with green peppers, onions, mushrooms and cheese, which was cooked just right, not too firm and not watery, but very cheesy. It was served with fried hash browns and crispy whole wheat toast, and a rich blend of full strength coffee, of course. It hit the spot and got my day off to a great start.

Homemade soup is included with all sandwiches and desserts (rice pudding, Jello and pies), which are also available sugar free.

Something I like about this place besides the convenient hours and the first rate service is the reasonable prices and the inclusion of sides with almost all orders. It just takes the guesswork out of my meal planning.

DINERS INFORMATION

Address
6888 Center St. – Rt. 615, Mentor, OH 44060

Phone
(440) 255-8810

Hours
Monday - Saturday, 6:00 a.m. – 9:00 p.m.
Sunday, 6:00 a.m. – 8:00 p.m.
Monday - Friday, 6:00 a.m. – 11:00 a.m. (Early Bird Favorie Breakfast)
Monday - Friday, 2:00 p.m. – 5:00 p.m. (Early Bird Dinner Special)

Price Range
$

Casa Fiesta

Not far from the shores of Sandusky, Casa Fiesta caters to those who have a taste for honest to goodness authentic Mexican cuisine. The building is hard to miss, not only because of its lemon yellow exterior that sharply contrasts with all that surrounds it, but also because there are two brightly colored palm trees in front that light up the night sky and glow like rockets. The fiesta spirit continues inside this spacious building as well, where attentive servers tend to every guest as they walk through the door and throughout their meal.

The menu is a cultural lesson that provides a glossary of Spanish terms, complete with pronunciation, for most of the items offered. However, for those of us who have rusty foreign language skills, English is the predominant language, which makes ordering pretty easy. Fortunately, most of the kind and patient servers speak English, too.

The specialty of the house over and above the 100 some items on the menu is the El Molcajete (sorry, no translation — this is one they missed in the glossary), which is grilled shrimp and diced ribeye steak with sautéed veggies (mushroom, belle peppers, and onions) in ranchera sauce and topped with mozzarella cheese. All is served in a hot bubbling molcajete. After looking up this term, I discovered that a molcajete is a deep ancient bowl used in preparing and serving food, sort of like the mortar of the mortar pestle

combination. This is truly an authentic Mexican dish.

Other favorites are the Wet Burrito (meat and beans wrapped in a tortilla shell and drenched in enchilada sauce), a unique combination of the Fajita Quesadilla (a tortilla stuffed with choice steak or chicken and veggies covered with the house melted cheese dip), the El Grande Burrito (a large burrito, with a generous amount of steak or chicken, beans, and topped with cheese), and the traditional Chimichanga dish (two chimichangas topped with a mixture of melted cheese, ranchera sauce, sour cream, guacamole, and lettuce). These are standard menu entrees but the "Create Your Favorite Meal" section allows guests to choose exactly what they want, including Vegetarian and Texas Combinations, as well as Vegetarian Fajitas. Full color pictures adorn the menu not only to whet the appetite but also to provide an idea how the dishes are served.

As I ate my Enchiladas Jalisco entre (three enchiladas topped with sauce, cheese and shredded pork), I noticed that the interior of the adjoining wall had a cement arched awning that spanned the entire width of the room and created the appearance of a vibrantly painted hacienda, sort of like a house inside of a house with tables and booths underneath the awning. Most charming indeed!

If eating under the stars is appealing, the sizeable outdoor patio accommodates about 120 patrons who can enjoy their meals and a favorite beverage from the outdoor bar.

Even before you arrive at your destination in Lake Erie or points beyond, this would be a perfect spot to jumpstart your fiesta.

DINERS INFORMATION

Address
344 Milan Ave., Norwalk, OH 44857

Phone
(419) 660-8085

Hours
Monday - Thursday, 11:00 a.m. – 10:00 p.m.
Friday - Saturday, 11:00 a.m. – 11:00 p.m.
Sunday, 11:00 a.m. – 9:00 p.m.

Price Range
$$

Chowder House Café

Cuyahoga Falls, OH

This restaurant was not too hard to find once I was in the neighborhood, considering the bright blue and yellow exterior with matching umbrellas on the patio tables. When I entered the front door, the walls looked like someone had been let loose with a paint brush, sparkles and beads and an endless imagination. Windows hung by the counter, stain glass was randomly mounted in the windows, and odds and ends were casually strewn wherever the artist's creative urge seemed to take him. The bright blue tables fit in perfectly with the walls though most anything would have complimented the host of colors that were splashed everywhere.

The owners, Louis and Kerry Prpich, who bought the place from an artist in 2009, were both busy serving tables and preparing for a special event that evening by making special chocolate, ice cream and whipped cream desserts in wine glasses that were very decorative. Once seated, I was impressed by the detailed menus that provided a complete description of each entry. Louis said that they are known for their Twisted Noodles, which is seared Ahi Tuna served over chilled sesame noodles with wasabi and yakitori

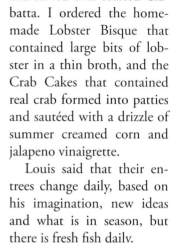

sauce. Scallop and Shrimp Bruschetta caught my eye especially sautéed with tomato, garlic, basil, olive oil and served over toasted Ciabatta. I ordered the homemade Lobster Bisque that contained large bits of lobster in a thin broth, and the Crab Cakes that contained real crab formed into patties and sautéed with a drizzle of summer creamed corn and jalapeno vinaigrette.

Louis said that their entrees change daily, based on his imagination, new ideas and what is in season, but there is fresh fish daily.

The big surprise, however, was when Kerry brought out the most scrumptious homemade banana chocolate cake that was at least eight inches high with chocolate sauce delicately dripped over the white icing. Absolutely delectable.

On the wall was a framed article that appeared in the Cleveland Plain Dealer about the restaurant entitled, "At Chowder House Café in Cuyahoga Falls, Delicious Food and Delightful Lunacy." I agree. It's short on frills, but long on creativity.

DINERS INFORMATION

Address
2028 Chestnut Blvd., Cuyahoga Falls, OH 44233
www.chowderhousecafe.com

Phone
(330) 794-7102

Hours
Monday - Friday, 11:00 a.m. (lunch and dinner)
Saturday, 5:00 p.m. (dinner)
Sunday, 10:00 a.m. – 2:00 p.m.

Price Range
$$

CW Burgersteins Great Sandwich Works

Wooster, OH

In 1984, brothers Greg and Todd Tieche developed a new restaurant to appeal to a more contemporary crowd, which was located in the finished lower level of the building shared with Melvin's and TJs. It was almost an immediate success and it provided an opportunity for up and coming comedians, like Drew Carey and Steve Harvey, to perform. Now it hosts local musicians on Thursday nights for Open Mic Night. Combined with its diversified menu, CWs is a fun place to get reputedly the "best wings in Wooster" as well as specialty sandwiches, gourmet burgers, generous salads, steaks and homemade desserts.

The menu is jam packed with more choices than the brain can absorb with the massive variety of items that are offered. Tops on the list are the wings, so I just had to try them. An order ranges from 10 wings to a crowd pleas-

ing 25 wings with a choice of sauce: tribe honey BBQ, totally teriyaki, mild, medium or hot, and wings of death. Being a rather conservative eater, I chose the tribe honey BBQ, which was just right in my book; not too spicy, but had enough flavor to enhance the tender meat. I'm no expert about wings, but maybe they are right. Maybe they do have the best wings in Wooster!

They also offer unique items like Mac & Cheese Bites, Buffalo Chicken Salad, The Dagwood Burger (double decker meat patty with bacon, grilled onions, sautéed mushrooms, banana peppers, chili and Swiss, American, provolone and bleu cheeses). Whew, what a mouth full! And despite the fact that this is casual dining at its finest, there are steaks and prime rib on the menu along with chicken and fish. If you still have room, there are home made desserts

No matter what, you won't go away hungry and on your way out the door take note of the hand cut tile mosaic of CW Burgerstein himself. The artisans who created this masterpiece were owner Greg Tieche's daughters, Abby and Ruth.

This is truly "The place to meet, eat, and share good times."

DINERS INFORMATION

Address
359 W. Liberty St., Wooster, OH 44691
www.tjsrestaurants.com/cws.htm

Phone
(330) 264-6263

Hours
Monday - Thursday, 3:00 p.m. – 11:00 p.m.
Friday - Saturday, 3:00 p.m. – Midnight

Price Range
$$

Doc's Deli

Mansfield, OH

At the corner of Poplar and Glessner Streets, about a half a block from Med Central Health System, sits a quaint little two-story brick house with a patio table out front and a large umbrella extended high in the air. The sign above the door reads "Doc's Soup Herb Deli". My first impression was that the owner could not make up his or her mind about the name, but I walked in anyway and was pleasantly greeted by a pristine deli complete with neat little tables with space saving chairs that push in and under the table and almost disappear. The full color pictures displayed behind the counter depicted a few tasty sandwich selections from the menu.

I ordered a grilled Corned Beef Panini with Swiss cheese on rye bread along with a bowl of Cream of Broccoli soup. The warmed sandwich melted the cheese and the Dijon mustard-mayo combination complimented the heaviness of the meat. The homemade soup was thick and rich with large

pieces of broccoli that tasted freshly picked. It was so good I wanted to order another bowl.

I met with Susan Vander Maas, the owner, who purchased the deli in 2007 and proceeded to renovate the building. She rebuilt the entrance with glass blocks, hung vertical blinds on the windows, added wood framed pictures on the newly painted walls and installed an eight foot coffee and condiment bar where guests can doctor their coffee or their sandwiches. After years of neglect, the place begged for a makeover to be completed before she could open for business.

When she did open she implemented a few innovative ideas not commonly found in any deli that I have visited. A customer could order a variety of freshly made sandwiches and bagged lunches from the menu. But Susan developed a system upon making your own sandwich from scratch starting with the bread choice (basil Focassia, Ciabatta roll, croissant, flat bread, etc.), moving on to the choice of meat (bacon, chicken breast, egg salad, pastrami, smoked ham, etc.) and cheese (American, cheddar, crumbled bleu, feta, Monterey jack, etc.), and finishing up with any extras (avocado, olives, pickles, pecans and a selection of sliced or chopped veggies). Not only can one make his or her own sandwich, but Susan has a database where the sandwich combo can be saved so that when the customer returns they can have that exact sandwich again, whether that is in a week or a year.

This is a most unique idea and I think Susan will go far in this business. She's built a unique place with excellent food.

DINERS INFORMATION

Address
424 Glessner Ave., Mansfield, OH 44903
www.docsdelimansfield.com

Phone
(419) 775-7775

Hours
Monday - Friday, 10:30 a.m. – 6:00 p.m.
Saturday, 10:30 a.m. – 3:00 p.m.

Price Range
$

Fairport Family Restaurant

Fairport Harbor, OH

Fairport Harbor is a sleepy town on the shores of Lake Erie. Despite all of the activity that surrounds the lake, this is a small stable area primarily influenced by the Hungarian population that lives there. There's nothing fancy about the restaurant in that it has the atmosphere of a café or diner, but the food is tasty and inexpensive.

The Hungarian influence is quite evident by the menu choices that include Hungarian Goulash, Cabbage Rolls, Stuffed Peppers, Corned Beef, and Chicken Paprikash. Of course, there are all time American favorites like Meatloaf and gravy, Beef Liver, Roast Beef and gravy, and Veal Cutlet. There are also daily specials that include Lake Perch, Strip Steak, Spaghetti and Meatballs, and Grilled BBQ Chicken. I found the Boneless Pork Chops very tender and perfectly complimented with applesauce and redskin potatoes. Most everything is homemade including salad dressings, soups, sauces and desserts.

I met with John Ritchie who along with his brother, Erik, owns the restaurant. And he told me that he has been in the restaurant business for more than a decade and serves as the chef while Erik "does everything else." The rest of the family also works in one capacity or another including John and Erik's mom, who makes the pies and cakes. Apparently they make a good team because the place is neat and clean, well maintained and was very busy while I was there. They have created a place that does not bear the high price of eating by the lake, which is just a block or two away, and provides a comfortable atmosphere.

Address
212 High St., Fairport Harbor, OH 44077

Phone
(440) 354-7474

Hours
Monday - Saturday, 7:00 a.m. – 8:00 p.m.
Sunday, 7:00 a.m. – 3:00 p.m.

Price Range
$

Melvin's Brick Oven & Bakery

Wooster, OH

This restaurant was the brainchild of Tom Tieche and his son Greg in 2002 and was an offshoot of TJs Restaurant in order to serve healthy international cuisine. It is located on the same floor but on the opposite side of the building from TJs, and the décor lends itself to a more laid back atmosphere. However, in season both restaurants share the spacious outdoor patio. Melvin's has a casual setting featuring a wood-burning brick oven where fresh baked breads and gourmet pizzas are prepared while diners look on.

The menu provides the diner with a unique choice of international favorites, and these items are expertly prepared by trained chefs that are skilled in

mixing herbs, spices and other items to create distinctive dishes. Stop by to savor some of these appetizers and entrees - Grecian Chicken Salad, Italian Sirloin Steak, Chicken Fettuccini Alfredo, Greek Hummus, Crab Rangoon,

Cheese Quesadilla and a Quesadilla Burger, Thai Lettuce Wraps and Thai Walnut Grouper, Oriental Potstickers, and Melvin's Bruschetta. There is also a great selection of pizza that can be topped with a variety of items, but those offered are the Basic Pizza with sun-dried tomatoes and portobella mushrooms, the Sicilian Pizza (spicy sausage, roasted red and green peppers and onions), Thai Chicken Pizza (chicken, bacon, scallions, carrots, red onion and spicy Thai sauce), and the Greek Pizza (fresh spinach, feta cheese, tomatoes, and calamata olives). All are finished off with either provolone or mozzarella cheese. The international flair influences the soups (homemade Hot Grecian Chicken Salad and French Onion), and a variety of sandwiches, wraps and paninis that provide a spark to any meal.

Of course, there are American favorites as well, so take time to study the menu before deciding and enjoy a cool drink on the patio.

DINERS INFORMATION

Address
359 W. Liberty St., Wooster, OH 44691
www.tjsrestaurants.com/melvins.htm

Phone
(330) 264-6263

Hours
Tuesday - Saturday, 4:00 p.m. – 9:30 p.m.
Closed Sunday

Price Range
$

Mohican Tavern

Loudonville, OH

This area is rich in history, which is reflected in the use of the Mohican reference in many area businesses and the proximity of the 1100-acre Mohican State Forest located just five miles out of Loudonville. Situated downtown, however, I found the 30-year-old Mohican Tavern to be a clean, rustic old building and the nicest restaurant in the area. Current owners Jim and Beth Gardner have bought and sold it a couple of times, but since returning to Loudonville they have settled in to enjoy the busyness of the place with their regular patrons and new visitors as well.

Bob Harpster greeted me and gave me a tour of the two-story restaurant, which has a most unique décor style. It has the usual booths and tables, but upon closer inspection of the brass colored walls I discovered that there were hundreds of license plates dating back to the 1920s through the 40s. From a distance they looked like embossed wall paper, but they were overlapped and long ago painted with a long wearing enamel finish when the restaurant was known as the Brass Plate. They were in remarkably good condition and cer-

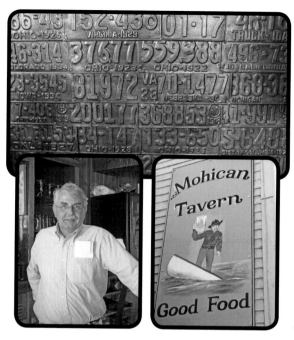

tainly have stood the test of time.

The menu features the all-American favorites of burgers (certified Angus meat products) and sandwiches of all sorts (Grilled Chicken Breast, Walleye), a daily create your own sandwich special and a variety of homemade soups. I also noticed a distinct German influence in items like the Potato Pierogies, Jumbo Bratwurst, and Steamed Sauerkraut, which Bob mentioned was due the local Amish community.

The dinner menu also offers Jumbo Lump Crab Cakes served with remoulade sauce, Char-gilled Chicken Pasta, Surf & Turf (6 oz. New York strip steak and crab cakes), and Boneless Pork Chops. Of course, there are many types of salads to choose from. Desserts are limited and usually feature cheesecake or peanut butter chocolate cake. Both hit the spot if you have room after a big meal.

After driving quite some distance from the southern counties, the sign "Mohican Inn – Good Food" was a welcome sight in this neck of the woods.

DINERS INFORMATION

Address
267 W. Main St., Loudonville, OH 44842

Phone
(419) 994-0079

Hours
Monday - Thursday, 11:00 a.m. – 9:00 p.m.
Friday - Saturday, 11:00 a.m. – 10:00 p.m.
Sunday, 11:00 a.m. – 6:00 p.m.

Price Range
$

Pickle Bill's on the Waterfront

Grand River, OH

Pickle Bill's has a long and interesting history dating back to 1967, when owner Jerry Gibson created a restaurant in Cleveland Flats by the same name. As a fan of the old time actor, W.C. Fields, Jerry took William Claude's shortened first name, Bill, and added "pickle" because of W.C.'s reputation for often being intoxicated. Jerry ended up with the unique name of Pickle Bill's, which he carried over to his restaurant's current location at River Street in Grand River. Field's silhouette has been adapted as the company logo and is prominently displayed on the establishment's signs and printed materials.

This restaurant has been a continuous building project starting with the original River Street place and eventually expanding with a Pilot House from a 1912 freight ship named the *Austin*, a 400 seat dock overlooking the river, a barge which is a carousel-like floating bar, and finally the Roof and Cantina bars which were added last. Despite all this talk about bars, an excellent variety of dishes are served

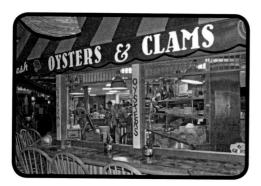

in each location of this family friendly place.

It has not been an easy time for Jerry, and in 1998 a blazing fire leveled Pickle Bill's to the ground. Not to be deterred, Jerry rebuilt and opened the new restaurant in January of 2000.

The décor is hard to describe and requires considerable time wandering around looking at the many oddly dressed mannequins, including a fully suited deep sea diver, the sea creatures, and an assortment of paraphernalia displayed in every nook and cranny. It is most fascinating to be sure and makes the dining experience one of a kind. It is part bedlam, part house of horrors, but totally fun!

Being on the waterfront has its advantages in that fish is readily available and constitutes the majority of the dishes served here. Fresh water haddock, perch and walleye, Atlantic salmon and swordfish, and shellfish including lobster, shrimp, oysters, mussels and clams abound. Though there are other seafood restaurants in the area, Pickle Bill's has a great reputation for excellent food in a unique atmosphere. Though many entrees are expensive, there are choices that are reasonably priced, so no matter what you order, it will be tasty and well-prepared.

DINERS INFORMATION

Address
101 River St., Grand River, OH 44045
www.picklebills.com
Call for the hours for the Barge and the Rooftop sections

Phone
(800) 352-6343

Hours
Tuesday - Thursday, Noon – 9:00 p.m.
Friday - Saturday, Noon – 10:00 p.m.
Sunday, Noon – 9:00 p.m.
Closed Monday

Price Range
$$$

The Pufferbelly Ltd.

As a landmark registered with the National Registry of Historic Places, the building in which The Pufferbelly restaurant is housed was a major railway depot and one of only two in the nation that features Tuscan Revival style architecture. It was on March 7, 1863, when the first passenger train of the Atlantic & Great Western Railroad reached the village of Kent, Ohio, thanks to Marvin Kent and his father, Zenas, who had obtained the state charter to allow railroad service to the village. It was certainly a day of celebration for the community, and service continued until Jan. 5, 1970, when the Erie Lackawanna Railroad discontinued passenger service after 107 years. The depot was purchased five years later, was fully restored and Pufferbelly's opened in 1981. Now it is not only a restaurant, but also offers a glimpse into the history of transportation in a bygone era.

Hung from the wall is an old poster announcing a Pancake Day held on April 6, 1976 at the depot, which I can only assume was a fundraiser for the restoration project. Train schedules and pictures of the depot in its

younger years are also displayed. However, what was astounding to me were the horse drawn carriage, a canoe and the cart overloaded with packages that are suspended from the ceiling. I prayed that the chains holding them would not break.

I was so enthralled in the history of this fascinating building that I almost forgot why I was there. The menu offerings are well balanced, and I enjoyed a number of samples. The Hot Artichoke Dip was baked with a tangy blend of chunks of artichoke hearts, melted cheese and unnamed herbs, and served with a mini French loaf of bread; just right with the dip. The Chicken Marsala was also quite tasty. The chicken breasts were sautéed until tender with mushrooms and scallions and then drenched with a rich Marsala mushroom sauce and served over angel hair pasta. The blend of the sauce with the chicken was spicy, but not overbearing. And the Cashew Chicken Croissant was a mixture of chunky chicken, crunchy cashews, and sweet mayonnaise all served with pita bread. It was just perfect with all of these textures coming together to form a true taste treat.

Just blocks from the Kent State University campus, Pufferbelly's is involved in the community and regularly features events that also spark the involvement of the Kent Chamber, Kent Historical Society and Rowe Museum, who are all housed in the old depot building. I concluded that there is good food, lots to see and fun things to do in this town.

Address
152 Franklin Ave., Kent, OH 44240
www.pufferbellyltd.com

Phone
(330) 673-1771

Hours
Tuesday - Thursday, 11:00 a.m. – 10:00 p.m.
Friday - Saturday, 11:00 a.m. – 11:00 p.m.
Sunday, 11:00 a.m. – 2:30 p.m. (brunch); 3:00 p.m. – 9:00 p.m. (dinner)
Winter hours Sunday and Monday closes at 8:00 p.m.

Price Range
$$

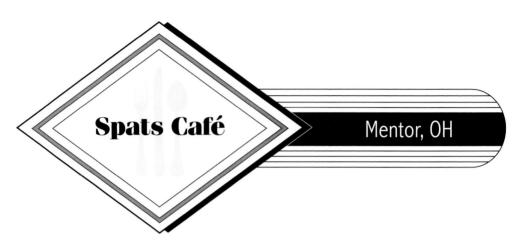

Spats Café

Mentor, OH

What a lovely place Penny and Paul Gamrut have created in a small strip mall off of the uniquely named Johnnycakes-Ridge Rd. This seems to be the Cheers place in Mentor because everyone knows everyone else, but it is a hang out for the whole family.

Part of the establishment is a spacious sports bar complete with televisions, booths, and stools at the expansive bar. The walls are decorated with flashy signs, daily specials, sports schedules and scores. The roomy covered patio, which is easily accessible from the small dining room inside, overlooks the surrounding area and draws color from the hanging plants. And then I was surprised to discover a substantial great room that serves as an overflow and it still provides a comfortable atmosphere. The size of this restaurant is certainly deceptive from the outside.

After more than three decades working in corporate America, Paul pursued his dream of owning a restaurant and worked at establishing it for five years before retiring for good from his primary job. Penny eventually resigned from her banking job and the Gamruts created a popular local Italian eatery which is influenced by Paul's mother who was a native of Italy and a "wonderful cook," according to Paul.

The menu features Spaghetti and Meatballs, Eggplant Parmesan, Lasagna, Ravioli, Carbonara and Cavatelli among other Italian specialties, which are often listed on the Nightly Specials along with all-you-can-eat Beer Battered Cod on Friday nights. They even offer home made Pierogies sautéed in butter with grilled onions and served with sour cream, just the way my grandmother made them. Absolutely delicious! Fried or broiled Lake Walleye or Perch and steamed mussels, as well as chicken and burgers are also popular offerings. And homemade fresh daily soups and sandwiches are available anytime, but are a staple on "The Super $3.95 Lunch" menu.

Bring the family and enjoy a good meal at a reasonable price. You won't be disappointed!

Address
9853 Johnnycakes-Ridge Rd., Mentor, OH 44060

Phone
(440) 352-0597

Hours
Monday - Saturday, 11:00 a.m. – 2:30 a.m.
Kitchen closes: Monday – Thursday, 10:00 p.m.
Friday - Saturday, 11:00 p.m.
Sunday, 9:00 p.m.

Price Range
$$

TJ's Restaurant

Wooster, OH

In 1964, Wooster was a struggling town and a mere shadow of what it is currently. Tom Tieche and Jack Clampitt recognized that there was no place in town to get a steak in a relaxed atmosphere. So the two local businessmen joined together to establish Tom and Jack's Lounge. Eventually, Jack sold his half of the restaurant and Todd Tieche joined his father Tom in the venture. Over the years three restaurants were born at the West Liberty Street location: TJ's Restaurant, Melvin's Brick Oven and CW Burgersteins. All have separate menus and appeal to different clientele.

TJ's provides fine dining in a casual atmosphere. It is a come as you are kind of place where one cannot only get a great steak, but other entrees as well. Blackened Grouper with Louisiana Shrimp Sauce and Sauteed Halibut top the list, but you cannot ignore the popular Naked Fish that features salmon, tilapia, grouper and mahi mahi served with spicy remoulade or orange tartar sauce, rice and the chef's selected vegetables. There is also an excel-

lent selection of pasta dishes using a unique blend of ingredients to satisfy even the most particular diner. A few of the selections are succulent Lobster and Asparagus Angel Hair in a light lemon cream sauce, Wild Mushroom, and Spinach in a tomato sauce served over and Whole Wheat Penne, Fettuccini topped with rich Alfredo sauce, and spicy Cajun Shrimp and Sausage. As if this weren't enough, there are also Blue Plate and Daily Specials, too. All bread and desserts are homemade and fresh out of the oven, but their specialty dessert is the Crème de Menthe Brownie. Layers of chocolate brownie is mixed with layers of crème de menthe frosting and topped with chocolate icing. It is served warm with mint ice cream and it is truly the best I have ever tasted.

If you are looking for affordable fine dining, this is the place.

DINERS INFORMATION

Address
359 W. Liberty St., Wooster, OH 44691
www.tjsrestaurants.com

Phone
(330) 264-6263

Hours
Monday - Friday, 11:00 a.m. – 9:00 p.m.
Saturday, 4:30 p.m. – 9:00 p.m.
Closed Sunday

Price Range
$$

CENTRAL WEST
REGION

Bel Lago Waterfront Bistro	Westerville, OH
Ben & Joy's Restaurant	Mt. Sterling, OH
The Bistro Off Broadway	Greenville, OH
Chattan Loch Bistro & Pub House	Bellefontaine, OH
Cherry Street Diner	Ashville, OH
CJ's Highmarks	Sidney, OH
Doubleday's Grill & Tavern	Centerville, OH
Fairlawn Steak House	Greenville, OH
Golden Nugget Pancake House	Dayton, OH
Goodwin's Family Restaurant	Circleville, OH
JR Hooks Café	Circleville, OH
LaPalma Mexican Restaurant	Bellefontaine, OH
Lindey's	Columbus, OH
Lost in the 50's Diner	St. Mary's, OH
Oscar's	Washington Court House, OH
Peach's Grill	Yellow Springs, OH
Pullman Bay	Celina, OH
The Purple Turtle Café & Bakery	Washington Court House, OH
The Refectory	Columbus, OH
Sweeney's Seafood House	Centerville, OH
Tuscan Table	Circleville, OH
Urbana Airport Café	Urbana, OH
Werner's Smokehouse	Jeffersonville, OH
Winds Café, Bakery and Wine Cellar	Yellow Springs, OH
Young's Jersey Dairy	Yellow Springs, OH

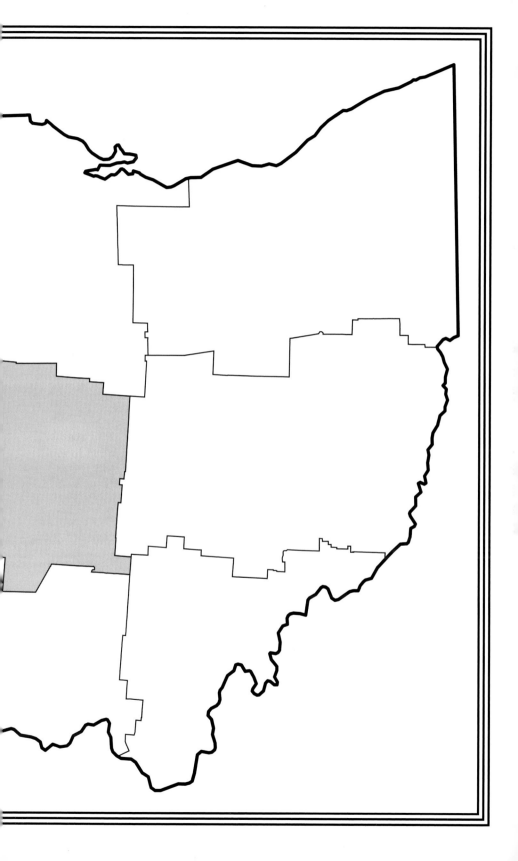

Bel Lago
Waterfront
Bistro

Westerville, OH

I had lived near Hoover Reservoir years ago and always thought that there should be a restaurant on the waterfront, especially when it is so busy with boaters and swimmers during the summer. Over the years, the area has developed significantly with sprawling housing developments, small strip shopping areas and docks dotted up and down the shoreline. Bel Lago is exactly what I had in mind way back when.

This Italian eatery features a scenic outdoor terrace, a spacious indoor dining room and a comfortable lower outdoor deck, all with a great view of the reservoir and shoreline. The design of the building is unique and utilizes nature as a backdrop. The interior is designed with an Italian flair, and the focal point in the dining room is a magnificent canopied bar with a vantage point that allows patrons to see the water outside and most of the dining room from where they are seated.

Both the lunch and dinner menus offer an assortment of popular appetizers – house Marinara Mussels, Sweet Pea Risotto Balls and Four Cheese Dip. The entrees include Italian Lasagna with freshly made meat sauce

and pasta, Spaghetti and Meatballs with marinara and home made meatballs, and Eggplant Parmesan with vegetable and parmesan risotto and topped with marinara and mozzarella. Mac and Cheese takes on a different twist when it is tossed with chunks of lobster meat and penne paste combined with a creamy white cheddar cheese sauce that proves to be an excellent mix, as I personally found out. Generous portions of fresh cut steaks are always a crowd pleaser and include Bone-in Black Angus Filet, New York Strip Steak and Pittsburgh Style Delmonica Steak. Being a native of Pittsburgh, the Delmonico is one of my favorites. And my husband, John, had the Blue Cheese Stuffed Filet with twice-baked potatoes and green beans with goat cheese, which he thoroughly enjoyed. A full complement of soups, salads, sandwiches and brick oven pizzas round out the offerings.

We both enjoyed the unique variety of Bel Lago desserts that include homemade Citris Cheesecake, Blueberry Crème Brulee, Triple Chocolate Fudge Cake, Tiramisu or Marshmallow Chocolate Cayenne Cake. Each bite of the samples was more heavenly than the last one, so I can't recommend which was the best. All were delicious.

This is a casually elegant restaurant, but with a fun and friendly atmosphere.

DINERS INFORMATION

Address
170 N. Sunbury Road, Westerville, OH 43801
www.bellagobistro.com

Phone
(614) 891-0200

Hours
Thursday, 11:00 a.m. – 10:00 p.m.
Friday - Saturday, 11:00 a.m. – 11:00 p.m.
Sunday - Wednesday, 11:00 a.m. – 9:00 p.m.

Price Range
$$$

Ben & Joy's Restaurant

Mt. Sterling, OH

In the heart of this small town with a population of about 1800, Ben & Joy's Restaurant has occupied the same location since 1984. During that time, thousands of travelers and area residents have walked through the door to enjoy a great cup of coffee with a homemade piece of pie or Joy's famous chicken and noodles or baked steak.

Together Ben and Joy managed this establishment until his death in 2003, and Joy has been handling it alone since, but she has had support and help from the community and her faithful employees. With three large rooms that sometimes fill up during busy times, Joy has had her hands full, but she knows that her customers are coming in for the "made from scratch" soups, chili, and cream pies. She even rolls out her own noodles with a pin.

In season, she buys produce from local farmers' markets to assure that she can provide garden fresh vegetables and fruits to her customers. And she keeps a good variety of choices on the daily buffet table including ribs, beef and

noodles, fried chicken, corn, applesauce and salad items. She truly has a servant's heart that she demonstrates through her dedication and the long hours that she spends bringing quality meals to her patrons, both regulars and others who are just passing through. The prices are reasonable and the food is just like my mom used to make.

She also has a hobby that she likes to share and that is collecting angels. In fact, she has dedicated a portion of her

restaurant to her Angel Room Gift Shop, where hundreds of angel statues keep watch over her. However, she encourages her visitors to buy one to take home with them. She has quite a collection, and some have been given to her by her customers, which are the ones she keeps, or she has found them in her travels, but it is a beautiful little shop to just wander through.

Homemade food, convenient location and at times live music as Joy rocks out on the piano and those who are willing join in with her in song are all great reasons to stop by. While you're there, say "Hi" to Joy for me!

Address
35 S. London St., Mt. Sterling, OH 43143
www.myplace.com

Phone
(740) 869-4324

Hours
Saturday - Thursday, 5:00 a.m. – 8:00 p.m.
Friday, 5:00 a.m. – 9:00 p.m.

Price Range
$

The Bistro
Off Broadway

Greenville, OH

I spoke with Lisa, the chef and manager, who was very accommodating. This is definitely a fun family place, with vintage toy planes suspended from the ceiling and a large collection of 1950s toy cars that toddlers of yesteryear used to pedal around. Old pressed metal tin tiles make up the ceiling and are painted black to bring down the ceiling, figuratively, since its height gives the impression of a large warehouse. But the numerous neon signs light up the place with a flash of pizzazz that injects a feeling of amusement far from the days of the Prohibition, when dimly lit night clubs and the 1940s' speakeasies were so prevalent.

The Amerbock Cheese dip, which was thick and slightly spicy, went well with the soft pretzel bites. Lisa's Own pan sautéed Crab Cakes topped

with a spicy remoulade sauce were delicious, but, once again, a bit too spicy for me, though some would think it not spicy enough. And the Prime Rib was prepared perfectly, tender, tasty, and juicy.

I found the service as well as the food to be excellent. The atmosphere was entertaining and would appeal to a couple just stopping by for dinner or a family needing a night out.

DINERS INFORMATION

Address
117 E. Fifth Street, Greenville, OH 45331
www.thebistrooffbroadway.com

Phone
(937) 316-5000

Hours
Tuesday - Friday, 11:00 a.m. – 2:00 p.m. (lunch)
Tuesday - Thursday, 4:00 p.m. – 9:00 p.m. (dinner)
Friday - Saturday, 4:00 p.m. – 10:00 p.m. (dinner)

Price Range
$$

Chattan Loch Bistro & Pub House

Bellefontaine, OH

T his is affordable dining at its finest, especially in a casual elegant atmosphere complete with black tablecloths. That statement sounds like a
contradiction, but in talking with owner Tracy McPherson, it makes perfect
sense. She opened this restaurant not only to "provide guests with the highest quality of service and value while maintaining our place in the community," as is stated in her mission on the menu, but "we commit to doing this
through…the employment and development of those with developmental
disabilities in a work environment of trust, loyalty and encouragement."

In other words, Tracy opened this restaurant in order to provide jobs and
the satisfaction and frustration attached with them to the developmentally
disabled in the community including her daughter, Leah, who I met when

I arrived. Having a developmentally disabled brother, I was so pleased that someone was thoughtful enough to step out and provide a safe and reassuring work place for those who are often shunned or, worse, ridiculed. Tracy's goal is honorable and begs to be respected and supported especially during these tough economic times.

In addition, Tracy is committed to provide menu selections that are "fresh, healthy options that taste great without lab-created substances added for flavor. We promote natural flavors and utilize a multitude of herbs and seasonings to give our menu a unique twist on traditional dishes." This goes for the homemade Chicken Salad, the 8 oz. Bacon Wrapped Filet Mignon, Smoked Gouda Pollo Vento Pasta, Angus certified burgers and Chicken Wings in the house signature sauces which are not only delicious, but cooked with the health and welfare of the diner in mind.

There are many other menu selections at Tracy's restaurant, named Chattan for her husband's family clan name in Scotland, and Loch, meaning lake, so no one should ever go away unsatisfied or hungry. Most of the soups, salads, sandwiches, steaks, chops, sides and desserts are homemade to assure quality.

In addition to a well balanced menu, Chattan Loch also sponsors special events like Wednesday night .49¢ Wings, $5 Burger Night every Thursday, Beer Club every 2nd Tuesday of the month, and the Wine Experience every 4th Tuesday. Live music is also featured most every Friday and Saturday along with monthly fundraiser events.

Tracy is a special person to take on such a responsibility, and Leah is a special and beautiful young lady, too. So when you are looking for a place to eat, stop by Chattan Loch Bistro. As the saying goes, "You'll be glad you did."

CENTRAL WEST

DINERS INFORMATION

Address
212 E. Columbus Ave., Bellefontaine, OH 43311
www.chattanloch.com

Phone
(937) 592-2696

Hours

Dining Hours: Monday - Friday, 11:00 a.m. – 2:00 p.m. (lunch)
Wednesday - Thursday, 5:00 p.m. – 9:00 p.m. (dinner)
Friday - Saturday, 5:00 p.m. – 10:00 p.m. (dinner)
Closed Sunday

Pub Hours: Wednesday - Thursday, 11:00 a.m. – 11:00 p.m.
Friday - Saturday, 11:00 a.m. – 1:00 a.m.

Price Range
$$

Cherry Street Diner

Ashville, OH

This is a charming diner located a block or so off Long Street in Ashville, but look for signs pointing the way because it is nestled on Cherry Street, which is a side street. Neat and clean with a down home décor, the atmosphere is warm and welcoming to all who come through the doors. Operating the diner for 19 years has allowed Pam Ward to get to know generations of Ashville residents, and she is now serving the grandchildren of neighbors she grew up with.

I was particularly impressed with her dedication, considering the long hours that she works. Unlike most jobs, arriving 15 to 30 minutes before start time is adequate, in the restaurant business when the doors open up at 6 a.m. as they do at Cherry Street, coffee has to be hot, eggs have to be cracked and sausage has to be sliced. That means that Pam and her staff have to be preparing food by about 4:30 a.m. Groan…that's way too early to start any day! However, I was pleased that she does have that commitment to provide her customers with great food day in and day out, because I was the beneficiary the day I visited.

The menu is not extensive, but it has the basic comfort food that should satisfy and fill. Entrees include a Shrimp Platter, Chopped Beef Steak, Pork Chops, Grilled Tenderloin and Fried Chicken, as well as a wide variety of sandwiches (chicken, fish, burgers, tenderloin, ham and cheese, BLTs, grilled cheese and hot dogs). Her daily specials fill the gap in her menu and provide more variety.

Each week is pretty much the same: Ham and Beans with cornbread, Liver and Onions, Chicken and Noodles, freshly made Chicken Salad and what Pam describes as a Split: a sandwich that is part turkey and part beef split down the middle and covered with gravy. Add mashed potatoes and it makes quite a tasty meal.

As I ate my turkey/beef split sandwich, I saw a rare sight outside the window. An albino squirrel appeared dashing across the grass and was pure white from head to toe. Pam wasn't surprised, because he pays a visit almost daily and loves to nibble on a slice of bread that she gives him by holding it between his paws. I was able to get a closer look at him as we went to the small building just a few feet from the restaurant. There we entered a small quaint gift shop that is chocked full of items made mostly by Pam's daughter. Most impressive is the quality of the workmanship and skill needed to produce such lovely gifts. I was tempted to start my Christmas shopping early. When you are visiting the Cherry Street Diner, stop by the gift shop too and buy something for someone special even if it is for yourself.

Address
29 Cherry Street, Ashville, OH 43103
Phone
(740) 983-9669
Hours
Daily, 6:00 a.m. – 2:00 p.m.
Price Range
$

CJ's Highmarks

Sidney, OH

This is truly a family restaurant that is encouraging to school children. In brainstorming the idea of the theme, the owner, John Iremshire, wanted to personalize the restaurant by incorporating unique items specific to the Sidney schools. He found a considerable amount of memorabilia, like pendants, trophies, plaques, diplomas and shirts to decorate with, so the place was transformed into a mock school complete with fake graffiti on the bathroom walls. Each of the three dining rooms has a different theme. I sat in the library, with neatly organized stacks of real books on shelves lining the walls and a stern librarian looking my way. She gave me the shivers, even though she was painted on the wall. I guess it brought back too many memories from school!

The name CJ's HighMarks is derived from the owner's philosophy of only having high marks in food and service, a belief that he still upholds. The food has a good reputation, because the ingredients are fresh and rarely frozen, and each recipe is prepared to order, not sitting under a heat lamp. Every breaded item is battered and dipped by hand, thus eliminating batter that is runny or too thick. Their rich brown gravy does not come from a jar or an envelope, but from the pot roast drippings like my grandma used to make. Fresh homemade banana nut and apple muffins are served warm at each table and have that melt in your mouth richness.

I was particularly impressed by the size of the menu and the wide variety of selections that would surely satisfy almost any taste. I was also pleased to learn that everything is made from scratch. I sampled their made fresh daily Chicken Cheese soup that had a creamy cheesy broth with large chunks of chicken. And the tender, meaty Philly Steak Sandwich had thinly sliced Prime Rib topped with grilled onions, peppers and Swiss cheese on a fresh hoagie roll. Pasta is popular and includes the Chicken Parmigiana, Cajun Chicken, Stuffed Chicken Scampi and the Creamy Broccoli Alfredo. There are also four selections of Burgers weighing in at a half a pound, as well as five selections of Steaks.

Overall, there is something for everyone...and if there is any whining you'll be sent to the principal's office!

CENTRAL WEST

DINERS INFORMATION

Address
2599 W. Michigan Ave., Sidney, OH 45365
www.cjhighmark.com

Phone
(937) 498-0072

Hours
Monday - Thursday, 11:00 a.m. – 10:00 p.m.
Friday - Saturday, 11:00 a.m. – 11:00 p.m.
Sunday, 9:00 a.m. – 9:00 p.m.

Price Range
$$

Doubleday's Grill & Tavern

Centerville, OH

Doubleday's was established in 1991 and named after the inventor of baseball, Abner Doubleday. At one point it was slated to be a sports bar, but eventually became more of a family place. This goal came into sharper focus when the Thomas family purchased Doubleday's in 1997. With three generations in the food industry, the family was capable of determining a need and successfully providing the right eatery to satisfy that niche market. When they purchased Doubleday's they wanted to provide a higher quality of food and service for area residents. Their sister restaurant, the Golden Nugget Pancake House, a well-established breakfast and lunch restaurant in Dayton, is also owned and managed by the Thomas family. Both operations have displayed a determination to satisfy their customers by providing the finest dishes with the freshest ingredients grown by local producers. The management also provides a favorable work environment for their staff, who are long termers and have been around for years.

Doubleday's serves lunch and dinner and caters to a bar crowd. The set up of the restaurant, however, is versatile, in that there are a number of televisions in the bar area where sports of all sorts can be viewed, and nearby

but separated from the bar are booths and tables where a couple can have a private conversation or a family can celebrate a special event.

Manager Jerry Gordon greeted us and made us feel right at home by providing generous samples of their most popular entrees. He started off with the Hat Trick. No, it isn't what you might think. Actually, this is a sandwich that has grilled turkey and Swiss cheese, bacon and tomato served on a pretzel bun, which is a soft salted bread. It was a little different, but tasty. The Corned Beef Reuben has a great combination of meat (choice of either corned beef or turkey), sauerkraut, Swiss cheese and homemade Thousand Island dressing. The Blackened Pork Chop was excellent, topped with melted bleu cheese and homemade onion straws. And the Monster Chocolate Chip Cookies and Brownies are made fresh every day. You can be sure that we didn't leave without them. They were mouthwatering and were still warm.

This is an exquisite establishment with an abundance of dark wood and stained glass that gives the place warmth and ambiance.

Address
199 E. Alex Bell Rd., Centerville, OH 45459
www.doubledaysgrillandtavern.com

Phone
(937) 436-4666

Hours
Monday - Thursday, 11:00 a.m. — 10:00 p.m.
Friday, 11:00 a.m. — 10:30 p.m.
Saturday, 11:00 a.m. — 10:00 p.m.
Sunday, 11:00 a.m. — 9:30 p.m.

Price Range
$$

Fairlawn Steak House

Greenville, OH

This well-maintained old building is located across from the Darke County fairgrounds on the edge of Greenville. Originally a coffee stop, it has been a restaurant since 1936 and served weary travelers on their way between Dayton and Greenville. Pat Foley and his wife, Kandy, are the present owners, but his family purchased the business in 1980. Except for attending college, he has been working there most of his life and is now head chef. Other family members are involved as well.

It was very busy on Friday night when I visited, but the service was still efficient and the food was delicious. The menu is varied with six selections of hand cut steaks (Filet Mignon, Been Tenderloin, New York Strip, T-Bone, Rib Eye, Top Butt) grilled to order on an upright broiler under an intense heat. The Broasted Chicken is always fresh, never frozen, and then breaded

and fried under pressure. And tender fresh pork chops, which are always in demand, are supplied by Winter's, a local butcher, as is the broasted chicken. Pat tries to use the freshest produce and often buys from truck patches in the summer, which he claims makes a difference in the homemade salsa.

Friday is often fish night, and the Grouper (a Fairlawn favorite), Broiled Whitefish (Filet of Icelandic Cod) or Cedar Plank Salmon (Broiled on a cedar plank) are all good choices. So is either the jumbo deep fried Gulf Shrimp or the Alaskan King Crab Legs steamed in the shell. Pat takes pride in his homemade salad dressings, soups (potato, veggie, chili).

The décor is like many neighborhood restaurants, nothing fancy, but very comfortable and if you are a regular, "everyone knows your name" like Cheers in Boston only on a smaller scale. Fairlawn is very family oriented, with kids dressed in their sports attire accompanied by their parents before and after local games. This is a "come as you are" kind of place, so come as you are when you are in the neighborhood.

DINERS INFORMATION

Address
925 Sweitzer Street, Greenville, OH 45331
Check them out on Facebook

Phone
(937) 548-2262

Hours
Monday - Saturday, 11:00 a.m. – 1:00 a.m.
Closed Sunday

Price Range
$$

Golden Nugget Pancake House

Dayton, OH

The Golden Nugget is a breakfast and lunch place where the selections seem to be endless. It's impressive that one restaurant can offer so many types of unrelated dishes, but the chef is versatile and knows how to cook according to the customer's wishes. There are abundant selections in each category, so let me share with you what they are.

There are ten types of pancakes (cinnamon, southern pecan, peanut butter chocolate chip and banana to name a few), five types of waffles (blueberry, strawberry, bacon, pecan and plain egg), seven types of egg and meat dishes (eggs with ham, bacon, sausage, Hormel cured ham, smoked sausage, Canadian bacon, and steak), 15 types of omelets (among them are bacon, sausage, western, Denver, and Mexican), 17 types of sandwiches, and four types of salads (Deluxe garden, chef, grilled chicken, and chicken tenders). Whew! And that doesn't count the side orders that can be included with each dish.

We sampled many of the above selections including a veggie omelet made with large chunks of broccoli, mushrooms, onions and Colby cheese. It was very tasty and when I pierced it with a fork the melted cheese just oozed out. That's what I call a perfect omelet. We also tried a blintz, which is a thin egg batter wrapped over a mixture of sour cream, cottage cheese, cinnamon and sugar. This mixture is so pleasing to the palate it is hard to describe. On the other hand, the strawberry roll up is similar to the blintz, but the batter is wrapped around the

strawberries instead and topped with a glaze and whipped cream. Yes, this was fantastic! Then there were the pancakes, the French toast and the fried mush. All were mouth watering. I even had a potato pancake, which was so good that it reminded me of the way my mother made them, and I thought hers were the best.

After this scrumptious feast, I realized why people are lined up out the door at all hours trying to get a seat. The Golden Nugget does a large volume of business, but they don't lose the personal connection with the customer, especially the regulars that come in almost every day.

The Thomas family owns and operates The Golden Nugget and after talking with Stacy, I realized that they are a very close-knit group, even though they work together every day. In fact, the family gets together each Sunday for dinner and to share the day. They are hard working and have persevered through the tough times, including a fire that totalled the restaurant, but they also celebrate the good times, too.

Whether it is breakfast or lunchtime, this is one restaurant you don't want to miss.

DINERS INFORMATION

Address
2932 S. Dixie Drive, Dayton, OH 45409
Phone
(937) 298-0138
Hours
Tuesday - Friday, 6:00 a.m. – 3:00 p.m.
Saturday, 6:00 a.m. – 3:30 p.m.
Sunday, 7:00 a.m. – 3:30 p.m.
Price Range
$

Goodwin's Family Restaurant

Circleville, OH

Established in 1979 by Art and Janet Goodwin, this restaurant is a mainstay in this community, where many employees have worked with the Goodwins for decades. Not only do they give scholarships to their staff, but also reward them with raises for their hard work and dedication, which is an employment benefit you don't see too often.

Goodwin's provides a well-balanced daily lunch and dinner buffet that features their famous Broasted Chicken, as well as a wide selection of side items and delicious desserts. A breakfast buffet is also available on weekends. But it is the broasted chicken, which is cooked to order, that brings customers coming back time and again. Art told me that they sell between 2500 to 3000 pieces each week, and take-out orders can run up to 100 pieces or more.

In addition to the buffets and the tender juicy broasted chicken, the menu features a varied selection of burgers (Super D, Big D and the Bacon BBQ Super D) with your choice of cheese, veggies, and sauces (except for the BBQ Super D). Other entrees include beef (top sirloin, chopped beef, and country fried steak), fish (ocean perch, pollock and cod) and seafood (shrimp and clams).

A meal without dessert is like three wheels on a car. You have just got to finish the meal right. Goodwin's features their scrumptious cherry and pecan pies with an optional helping of ice cream piled high, as well as their fresh cream pies (chocolate, coconut and lemon) and their explosively delicious huge creamy cream puff.

You are sure not to leave hungry.

Box lunches are also available for those on the go. And with each sandwich or side dish purchased for carry out, you get a free drink. Now you can't beat that.

Finally, for those times when you want to get together with friends or business associates, a spacious game room that can accommodate up to 50 is also available for gatherings, meetings or for the Big Game and features a 42" flat screen TV, and free Wi-fi connection.

DINERS INFORMATION

Address
214 Lancaster Pike, Rt. 22 East, Circleville, OH 43113
www.goodwinsfamilyrestaurant.com

Phone
(740) 474-1845

Hours
Daily, 8:00 a.m. – 9:00 p.m.

Price Range
$

J.R. Hooks Café

Circleville, OH

My husband and I have been eating at Hooks for years and have always left satisfied and pleased with the quality of food. For a modest-sized town, Circleville is fortunate to have a restaurant such as Hooks with a reputation for excellence.

The décor is appealing and the division between the bar and the dining area provides privacy while eating or while watching the latest game in the bar with friends. Service has always been efficient and pleasant in a casual atmosphere that provides fine dining. My only recommendation would be to have more parking which is limited, with a few spaces in their lot or on the street. However, I have never left because I could not find a spot.

The menu focuses on all American favorites such as Bayou Chicken Florentine, New Orleans Fricassee, Cajun Meatloaf, Hunter Chicken, Apple Brandy Pork Chops, Beer Baked Ribs, and Shrimp & Grits. But for an international taste there is Roasted Salmon Linguine, Ribeye au Poivre, Sicilian Chicken Linguine and Boudin Balls.

My favorite is the Herb Cheese Mushrooms or the homemade Crab Chowder to start with, and then move on to the Jambalaya, which is a delicious mixture of shrimp, sausage, chicken and rice in an authentic knock your socks off Creole sauce of tomato, onion, peppers, celery, garlic, thyme and oregano. Par excellence!

Live music is regularly offered in the Music Room at Hooks that is connected to but acoustically separate from the main dining room. Guests can enjoy a meal while listening to talented local and national singers and musicians who perform a variety of music including jazz, blues, folk, Appalachian and Irish Celtic.

This is a restaurant with a style and grace all its own.

DINERS INFORMATION

Address
115 Watt Street, Circleville, OH 43113
www.jrhooksrestaurant.com

Phone
(740) 474-2158

Hours
Monday - Thursday, 11:00 a.m. – 10:00 p.m.
Friday, 11:00 a.m. – 11:00 p.m.
Saturday, 9:00 a.m. – 11:00 p.m.

Price Range
$$

La Palma Mexican Restaurant

Bellefontaine, OH

ocated near a busy shopping area on the outskirts of town, La Palma is a bright spot in an otherwise sea of fast food restaurants and chains. Owner Gustavo Ramirez impressed me as a hard working and dedicated man who is striving to provide for his young family. From what I observed he had all the right ingredients for a good business: a pristine establishment, a winning attitude, great staff and a high quality food. As soon as I sat down the server brought chips and salsa and took my order, which was a #33 – the Fajita Quesadilla Texana. It was promptly delivered and I enjoyed the combination of chicken, steak and shrimp, bell peppers, onions, tomatoes and cheese placed on a giant floured tortilla and expertly rolled. It was more than I could eat at one sitting, so I had the remainder boxed up for later. It was also served with beans, rice and a salad — quite a bit of food.

He mentioned that the other specials were the Fajitas, that are served on a sizzling platter with a variety of veggies and seasoned with a combination of spices. The Enchiladas come in four ways, and the Steak Mexicano is a sirloin steak cooked with tomatoes, onions and peppers. The Chimichangas are stuffed with chicken, beef or beans with rice. And the popular Combination meals usually include some combination of enchiladas, burritos, tacos, and quesadillas. Occasionally, the Vegetarian menu is appealing to someone watching their nutritional intake. And the Children's Plate has more variety on it than any I have ever seen.

The desserts are delectable, including the Sopapilla with Ice Cream, Fried Ice Cream, Cheesecake, Mexican Churros and the Flan that is the traditional Mexico City-style cream caramel baked fresh daily.

Overall, La Palma serves generous portions of excellent food in a colorful, pleasant atmosphere.

Address
2201 S. Main St., Bellefontaine, OH 43311
www.lapalmabarandgrill.com

Phone
(937) 652-4999

Hours
Sunday - Thursday, 11:00 a.m. – 10:00 p.m.
Friday - Saturday, 11:00 a.m. – 11:00 p.m.

Price Range
$$

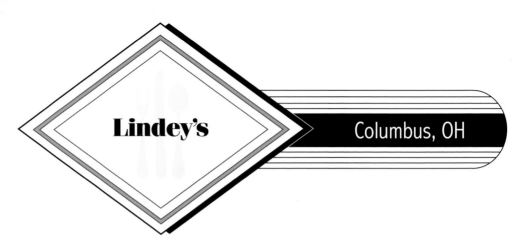

Lindey's

Considered to be one of Columbus's Top Ten restaurants, Lindey's is located in the heart of historic German Village, just a few blocks south of downtown, where old world charm is found in unique shops and boutiques, and a myriad of ethnic restaurants. Lindey's is a long-time favorite of mine because of the excellent service and fine food. It is a white tablecloth restaurant with a sophisticated atmosphere, but there is a casual "come as you are" attitude that prevails. Guests in tuxedos and long gowns, as well as Docker's and button down shirts sit in the same dining room. According to owner Sue Doody, "There is no dress code, because it is a place for everyone."

This 1800s era, three story Victorian building provides diversity throughout in that there is casual dining in the bar area, elegant dining in the main dining room, and relaxed socializing on the large patio that features a beautiful covered bar. No matter what part of the building you have settled in,

the servers are attentive to your needs.

Sue Doody purchased the former Lindenhof Restaurant in 1981 and changed the name to set a new start for this old eatery. She lovingly restored it, renamed it and swung open the doors to let the world in…and in they have come for the past 30 years. German Village was thriving in the mid-1800s to the early 1900s, and through Dodd's efforts there is hope that someday that era will return. She also supports the creative community in which the restaurant is located, and displays local artists' work throughout the restaurant. Jazz musicians are also featured once the patio is closed and everything moves indoors for the winter.

My visit began with a cup of Lobster Bisque topped with shrimp that was exquisite…rich and hardy, and full of flavor. Next, I had the Nut Crusted Chicken Salad with mixed greens, topped with apples, tomato, Applewood bacon, shredded Gouda cheese and drizzled with warm honey mustard dressing, which was superb. And as my entrée, I delighted in sampling the Tournedo of Beef, which is a single 4 oz. filet with Bearnaise, creamy garlic whipped potatoes and tender asparagus. You can be sure that I savored every bite.

I have always enjoyed the atmosphere here because it is relaxed and peaceful, not stuffy or stifling, and there is a creative buzz that seems to permeate the air, along with a variety of interesting guests.

CENTRAL WEST

DINERS INFORMATION

Address
169 E. Beck St. (Beck & Mohawk Streets), Columbus, OH 43215
www.lindeys.com

Phone
(614) 228-4343

Hours
Sunday - Thursday, 11:00 a.m. – 10:00 p.m.
Friday - Saturday, 11:00 a.m. – 11:00 p.m.

Price Range
$$$

Lost in the 50's Diner

St. Mary's, OH

"A dining experience that will take you back."

This is a fascinating place because it is more than just a diner; it is a destination spot. You not only can get a decent meal here, but you can spend half a day stepping back into the 50s by visiting the museum that Rick Francis has created. There are thousands of pieces of memorabilia, large and small, that serves as a trip down memory lane for anyone who lived during that era and a view of what life was like way back then for those who were born later. It's fun for everyone.

Rick had an occupation that was unrelated to the 50s, that took him all over the country, and for 23 years he picked up a vast amount of memorabilia and met many interesting people. One of those people was the unpublicized biological son of Elvis Presley by the name of, what else, Elvis Aaron

Presley Jr., who has laid legal claim to the name. Jr. has become a good friend of Rick's and regularly performs at the Lost in the 50's restaurant and museum. These performances and other events are listed on the web site.

The diner is set up in a 50s décor and looks like a set out of the *Happy Days* TV show. The usual diner food is featured, but there are a few homemade "Blue Plate Specials" that are worth checking out, such as Spaghetti and Meatballs, Country Fried Steak, hand breaded grilled Tenderloin, and Beef or Chicken and Noodles. Chicken is popular whether it is fried, grilled, broasted, tenders or in salad. And beef is closely behind with Black Angus steaks (sirloin, ribeye, or chopped sirloin) and burgers.

And what is a 50s diner without the old fashioned milk shakes served in large stainless steel cups or a banana split complete with three scoops of ice cream and a choice of chocolate, butterscotch or strawberry topping, nuts, real whipped cream and a cherry on top. Just like the "olden days."

This is a fun place to visit, whether you are eating or touring the museum or both. And it is perfect for the whole family.

CENTRAL WEST

DINERS INFORMATION

Address
1533 Celina Rd., St. Mary's, OH 45885
www.lostinthe50sdiner.com

Phone
(419) 394-4959

Hours
Sunday - Thursday, 8:00 a.m. – 8:00 p.m.
Friday - Saturday, 8:00 a.m. – 9:00 p.m.
Sunday, 8:00 a.m. – 1:00 p.m.

Price Range
$

Oscar's

Washington Court House, OH

L ocated in the heart of downtown Washington Court House, Oscar's is an unexpected surprise. From the street the exterior suggests an old 1890s movie marquee when the establishment was known as the Roxy Theater, but once inside the picture changes. Elegant tables with white tablecloths greeted me and the fragrance of fresh flowers complimented the aromas rising from the daily buffet lined up like soldiers in silver serving dishes. I met with Jason, co-owner with Nathan, and asked him how they arrived at the name for this New York style restaurant. He said it was named after Oscar Tschirky, the maitre d' who had defined the concept of casual elegance at the Waldorf Astoria in New York City. Together, Jason Gilmore and Nathan Zukowitz captured the New York idea in this small town.

Though Oscar's has an air of refinement, dress is casual and Jason, who trained at St. Clair Culinary School, said, "Everyone is welcome whether they're wearing jeans or formal dress." The American cuisine not only satisfies simple tastes, but those with discerning taste as well. Lunch, which is reasonably priced, offers gnocchi, potato dumplings with red marinara sauce, mac and cheese, sweet and sour meatloaf, and a variety of homemade desserts

such as New York cheesecake, coconut cake, bread pudding and a host of pies. Dinner from Tuesday through Thursday expands the menu and the Friday and Saturday dinner buffet includes seafood such as shrimp scampi, baked cod, fried fish,

crab cakes, filet and other steak selections. I enjoyed the julienne cheese potatoes, the roast pork and gravy, and the Shepherd's pie and each dish suited my taste to a T. Everything is made from scratch daily by Nathan. The young owners had catered special events for years and finally followed up on the many suggestions they received to open their own restaurant. They still cater, but their main focus is the restaurant, which is a delightful experience.

DINERS INFORMATION

Address
240 E. Court Street, Washington Court House, OH 43160

Phone
(740) 335-1036

Hours
Tuesday - Sunday, 11:00 a.m. – 2:00 p.m. (lunch); 5:00 p.m. – 8:00 p.m. (dinner)
Closed Monday
Specialties: Traditional American Homestyle

Price Range
$$

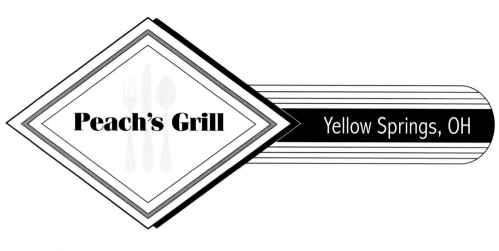

Peach's Grill

Yellow Springs, OH

Don Beard bought this drive-through/carry-out in 1997 and four years later renovated it to become a large casual dining restaurant. The drive-through was no more when a patio replaced the in-lane and a kitchen was added where the beer coolers had once stood. Two beautiful antique oak bars were eventually installed to accommodate the crowd that pushes in to hear live music over the weekend. A variety of microbrews are available along with 20 beers on draft and a wide selection of wines. The décor is colorful and contemporary, with dancing images painted on the walls. The atmosphere is charged with fun especially on Open Mike Night, when local talent is featured on the stage and an influx of guests come to party in this college town.

"Simple Food for a Complex Community," is Peach's slogan and refers to the diverse community in which it is a part. Antioch College students and faculty, visitors to the area, and the town's residents intermingle at Peach's to enjoy a variety of mostly home made specialties. I tried the Spinach and Artichoke dip with crispy deep fried pita chips (they come grilled too), a delicious sampler of wings with a variety of sauces, cheesy nachos topped with black beans and olives, tomatoes, and jalapenos. Their staple is beans and rice, which is included with many entrees. And the sun dried tomato feta and chicken salad in a

wrap served with grapes, nuts and celery was delightful. The homemade tortilla soup was hearty with a rich beefy taste, which I thoroughly enjoyed.

Located next to the Chamber of Commerce building, this is a fun place with upbeat music, belly filling food and excellent service.

DINERS INFORMATION

Address
104 Xenia Ave., Yellow Springs, OH 45387
www.peachsgrill.com

Phone
(937) 767-4850

Hours
Daily, 11:00 a.m. – 9:00 p.m.
Specialties: Mexican & American / Cheeseburgers

Price Range
$

Pullman Bay

Celina, OH

What a great location for a restaurant…right on the shore of Grand Lake St. Mary's where you can gaze across the lake as you dine. Perfect! Well, except for the parking. Not much room and you have to be careful not to back into anyone, but once in the door at Pullman's…well, there really isn't much room in the restaurant either. It's a pretty tight squeeze with the front door almost opening up into the kitchen. And it's first come, first serve, so no reservations accepted. But aside from all of that, the food is outstanding and they serve breakfast almost all day, along with lunch and dinner.

The menu is thematic, with some items named after railroad related references, like Dining Car Continental (fresh baked sweet roll with coffee), the Trolley Car Special (two eggs, toast and jelly), Market Street Special (chopped steak, two eggs and home fries). They are all special.

Some of the other popular items are Broasted Chicken, the Potato Works and the homemade soups and pies. The creamy potato soup is delicious, but

no matter who you ask, the pies are absolutely scrumptious (coconut cream, custard and fruit). From all sources, they are reputed to be excellent.

I spoke with owner Mike Wagner, who was busy cooking, delivering food and even cleaning up a few tables, but he took a few moments to tell me about the specials and how long he has owned the place (since 1984). During the course of the conversation, he also mentioned that he had gotten married the day before, on July 1. On July 2, he and his new wife were working together in the restaurant. Now that's dedication.

When you stop by to pick up a piece of pie, remember to congratulate them!

DINERS INFORMATION

Address
117 Lake Shore Dr., Celina, OH 45822
Phone
(419) 586-1664
Hours
Daily, 7:00 a.m. – 9:00 p.m. (summer)
Call for winter hours
Price Range
$

The Purple Turtle Café & Bakery

Washington Court House, OH

If you are looking for homemade healthy food, The Purple Turtle is just the right place. Brandon and Tia Long have been the proprietors of this well-kept secret since June 2009 and have created an excellent menu of scrumptious entrees, delectable desserts, hardy bread and flaky pastries. The atmosphere is laid back and conducive to slowing down life's pace a bit. The rustic setting with an Argentinean flare is small, but cozy, with seating only for about 28 plus a few more on the overstuffed couches that allow for a little down time. Nearby tables are set up to start a card game or read a good book. Live music entertains guests regularly.

Everything is made from scratch with the healthiest ingredients that the owners can find. Unbleached flour purchased from the Mennonite market, veggies in season from the farmer's market, organic milk, homemade cream with no additives and locally available coffee may shock the taste buds with their natural healthful flavor. The Stromboli is their signature sandwich on homemade bread and every bit of this large sandwich was very tasty. The thick rich Taco soup was the best I've ever tasted as was the cheesy black bean tortilla and the spinach artichoke dip with homemade chips for dipping.

Then there are the desserts. I started with a rich

black raspberry chocolate scone, moved on to the delicate vanilla cream puff and finished up this sugar high with the Media Luna Croissant (a puff pastry with a sweetened glaze). All desserts, breads, pastries and most everything else is made right in the restaurant by Brandon.

Wash down a fine meal with warm homemade Chai made with whole milk. This is a great place to eat, but even more a great place to hang out, work on the laptop or chat with friends.

Tia and Brandon are very creative and appear to be very compatible for a couple working so closely together every day.

Address
249 E. Court Street, Washington Court House, OH 43160
Check them out on Facebook

Phone
(740) 636-0950

Hours
Tuesday - Thursday	8:00 a.m. – 4:00 p.m.
Saturday	11:00 a.m. – 2:00 p.m.
Closed Monday	

Price Range
$

The Refectory

Columbus, OH

This is the essence of fine dining. Everyone should have a place where they can celebrate special occasions with style and grace, and create memories for the whole family. The Refectory happens to be my preferred place where my family has many good memories of anniversaries, birthday parties, engagement announcements, and new jobs. The elegance of this converted 1850s church with sparkling stained glass windows, high-beamed ceilings and mock candlelight still exists today despite many renovations.

In 1976, the transformation that eventually became The Refectory began and would result in a masterful piece of work architecturally speaking blended with the mastery in the kitchen.

If you are not used to lots of pampering and an excessive amount of attention from your server, it might take some getting used to, but it certainly is enjoyable to know that behind the scenes your entire meal, including what silverware will go with what course, is being orchestrated and paced like the Metropolitan opera.

The hors d' oeuvres the evening of our visit consisted of the Salmon Duet (cold salmon and hot smoked Salmon garnished with a dollop of caviar) was very delicate and a rich blend. The Mussel Soupe with shallots in a saffron cream had a subtle flavor

that soothed my palate. The main course consisted of the roasted Baby Rack of Lamb with parsley garlic that was so tender I could gently slice it with my fork. And, finally, for dessert I ordered the Crème Brulee with the crispy Palmier, which is a butterfly-shaped puff pastry cookie that is a perfect accompaniment to a rich crème brulée. If you wish to compliment your dinner with a glass of wine, the server will suggest the appropriate one from the restaurant's collection of over 700 wines.

The Refectory has an excellent reputation for impeccable service, and the finest of cuisine.

DINERS INFORMATION

Address
1092 Bethel Road, Columbus, OH 43220
www.therefectoryrestaurant.com

Phone
(614) 451-9774

Hours
Monday - Saturday, 5:30 a.m. – 9:00 p.m.
Closed Sunday
Specialties: Classic and contemporary French cuisine

Price Range
$$$

Sweeney's Seafood House

Centerville, OH

Sweeney's has been a part of the fabric of the Centerville community since 1994, when Ron Sweeney opened the doors of this New England style restaurant. He eventually moved to this area to enjoy the casual atmosphere of Centerville and also to be closer to his new establishment.

The nautical décor reinforces the New England influence, beginning with the red and white sail mounted to the ceiling and the 600 gallons of saltwater aquariums surrounding the dining area. Maritime pictures and other related items are also strategically placed around the restaurant. Of course, the menu includes selections of fresh seafood, but also chicken, steak, salads, pasta and sandwiches.

I started with the Clam Chowder, which was insanely good with chunks of clams in a rich creamy broth. The Seafood Gumbo, on the other hand, is made with large whole shrimp, rice and celery, but a bit too spicy for my liking. Next, I tried the grilled Norwegian Salmon topped with a horseradish crust and Dijon sauce, which was not as spicy or as hot as I anticipated. The salmon was grilled to perfection, though it can be ordered blackened or broiled,

and it was tender enough to just cut with a fork. I moved on to a sample of the Black n' Blue Scallops that combine blackened scallops and bleu cheese that are served over mesculin and topped with a Greek vinaigrette, which was refreshing compared to the creamy dressing that I usually get. Though my tank was filling up I had to try the authentic New York Cheesecake, which is made from scratch and topped with a brûlée or caramelized sugar (my favorite topping). Surprisingly, it was light and creamy though very rich, but it was worth it.

I enjoyed the relaxed atmosphere that was influenced by the fish swimming in the tanks by my booth. If you are into seafood, you will certainly enjoy the selections that Sweeney's has to offer along with the ambiance of the place. Though the restaurant is on the corner, there is plenty of parking behind the building.

Address
28 W. Franklin St., Centerville, OH 45459
www.sweeneysseafood.com

Phone
(937) 291-3474

Hours
Tuesday - Thursday, 11:30 a.m. – 9:30 p.m.
Friday, 11:30 a.m. – 10:30 p.m.
Saturday, 5:00 p.m. – 10:30 p.m.
Sunday, 5:00 p.m. – 8:30 p.m.
Closed Monday

Price Range
$$

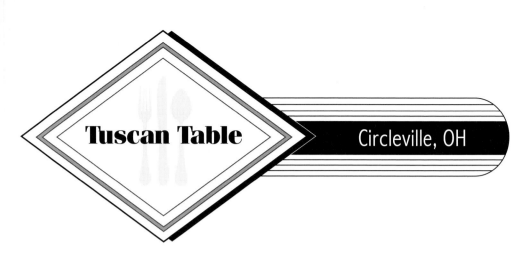

Tuscan Table

Circleville, OH

As their motto reflects – *"A Casual Family Friendly Italian Restaurant"* – this is the place for Italian food served in a family setting with that Tuscan flare. General Manager Jennifer Rieder warmly greeted me and provided me with the background of this Italian gem in downtown Circleville, not far from St. Rt. 23. And as I sipped my iced tea, I was fascinated by the efficiency of the chef who prepared dishes just yards away from my table. I saw the Mile High Lasagna as it came out of the oven and though slightly exaggerated (not quite a mile high), it is more than enough food. Portions of the "made from scratch" Spaghetti and Meatballs with the chef's homemade sauce were also generous and piled high on the plates. And the aroma from the stone-fired pizza was enticing. Tuscan Table is well known for its hand-crafted pastas, sandwiches and fresh soups.

I tried the Chicken Milanese, which is a lightly browned boneless chicken breast finished with homemade alfredo and lemon juice and served with red skin potatoes and vegetables in season. The chicken was tender and the al-

fredo was creamy and insanely good. The stuffed mushrooms, which are my weakness, were also excellent. Other specialties that bring patrons in from far and wide are the Blackened Chicken Fettuccine with a spicy kick, the Shrimp Pomodoro, Clams Fettuccine, and the Veal, which is made in a variety of ways including Veal Parmesan, Marsala, Piccatoa or Saltimbocca. The chicken can also be prepared in any of these dishes as well. There are also grilled specialties like Salmon Florentine, Pork Chops and Filet Mignon.

As a family friendly place, the Build Your Own Pizza is popular with a choice of sauces, cheese, meats and vegetables.

In addition to fine food, Tuscan Table also sponsors regular events and is involved in the famous Pumpkin Show each October. So come on in when you're in town or just passing through. You will certainly enjoy your visit!

Address
122 N. Court Street, Circleville, OH 43113
www.the-tuscantable.com

Phone
(740) 477-3040

Hours
Sunday - Thursday, 11:00 a.m. – 10:00 p.m.
Friday - Saturday, 11:00 a.m. – Midnight

Price Range
$$

Urbana Airport Café

Urbana, OH

Years ago when we owned our own plane, my husband, John, and I would fly to Urbana quite often just to have coffee and a piece of delicious homemade pie. It was very convenient to land, park the plane outside the door and walk right in and have breakfast or lunch, too. I was pleased to find that not much has changed over the years. The down to earth, good American home cooking that we enjoyed way back when is still on the menu. It may be even better now because some items are of higher quality. For instance, heart healthy, locally raised Buffalo burgers are now available and the beef comes from a nearby farm. Of course, there are Luncheon Specials that fill the void like Beef and Turkey served with mashed potatoes and gravy, a Chicken Salad Plate with fruit, Chef's Salad, Baked Swiss Steak, Beef and Noodles and a variety of seasonal homemade soups (cream of broccoli, chicken gumbo, chicken noodle, vegetable, bean and chili).

What the Airport Café has always been known for, however, is their daily freshly baked pies. The endless list includes fruit pies (cherry, apple, peach, rhubarb, black raspberry) as well as cream pies and even peanut butter. There

is certainly a favorite flavor to please everyone's palate.

The restaurant changed ownership back in 2004, but it remained in the family. Pat Hall had owned it for almost 20 years and was not only responsible for day-to-day operations, but she also baked those fabulous pies. She eventually sold the business to her son, Doug, and his wife, Michelle, but thankfully Pat is still in the pie business. In fact, the Café was featured in an article in *Country Living* magazine.

Whether you fly in or drive in — yes, there is a spacious parking lot — this is one of the more interesting places to eat not only because you can watch the activity at the airport and planes taking off and landing, but you can meet new people who are coming and going.

Nearby is a new museum dedicated to WWII aircraft and their pilots.

DINERS INFORMATION

Address
1636 W. Main Street, Urbana, OH 43078
Phone
(937) 652-2010
Hours
Tuesday - Saturday, 7:00 a.m. – 7:30 p.m.
Sunday, 8:00 a.m. – 2:30 p.m.
Closed Monday
Price Range
$

Werner's Smokehouse

Jeffersonville, OH

Marsha Arnold, daughter of owners Rich and Barb Werner, and restaurant manager, was one of the most knowledgeable managers I have met. Her 4-H experience raising and showing hogs along with her college Ag degree provided her with an excellent basis for this business. Because of her exposure in the restaurant she has learned how to prepare a variety of dishes and said that they enjoy these hardy animals both on and off the hoof. She manages every aspect of this fine BBQ place. Werner's Smokehouse is appropriately named considering that there is a large smoker in the rear parking lot where all of the smoked meats are cured for hours.

Marsha is very particular about the meat she serves and insists that it is as fresh as possible. All the meat is smoked on the premises, hand cut and cooked to order. I can confirm that the meat is tender, the sauce is rich with a tasty blend of spices and other ingredients that make up the famous Werner's BBQ sauce, and have been perfected over the years. I particularly enjoyed the "cut with a fork" butterfly pork chops dipped in sauce. Both the

pulled pork and the hog wings (the bottom of the shank of a ham that is smoked, fried and then grilled) are cooked to perfection. And the baby back ribs are seasoned with a special rub, smoked for about 90 minutes to capture that subtle smoke flavor and then glazed in sauce. The Hickory Smoked Chicken Breast is golden brown and tender, served with the choice of Italian or BBQ sauce. Other meats that are slow smoked are hand sliced Beef Brisket and grilled Ham Steak. All meals come with homemade sides like cole slaw, thin and delicious crispy Saratoga Chips. Our meal was delicious and included crunchy Sweet Potato Chips with brown sugar and cinnamon

The wide variety of homemade desserts are sure to satisfy the sweet tooth, especially pies like peanut butter, pecan, coconut cream, chocolate moose and the fruit pies, too. Special desserts regularly available are bread pudding and carrot cake.

Conveniently located near the interchange of St. Rt. 35 and I-71, and across from the sprawling Prime Factory Outlet Stores at Jeffersonville, Werner's not only caters to guests visiting their restaurant, but also those who are staying in the area. They deliver complete meals, special orders and bulk food for larger groups to hotels and motels located nearby.

If you are a BBQ fan, you will not be disappointed when you eat here.

DINERS INFORMATION

Address
11396 Allen Rd., Jeffersonville, OH 43128
www.wernersbbq.com

Phone
(740) 948-2989

Hours
Daily, 11:00 a.m. – 9:00 p.m.

Price Range
$$

Winds Café, Bakery & Wine Cellar

Located in downtown Yellow Springs, just blocks from Antioch University and surrounded by unique shops and boutiques, Winds is a breath of fresh air in that it provides a relaxed atmosphere with an elegant flare. White cloth napkins complement the dark wood tables and fresh flowers grace each table that lends a special stylishness I did not expect in this college environment. The dining area is well designed with partial walls erected to provide privacy in an open environment, and the bar area is set off to one side of the restaurant, which creates a more intimate environment. A working fireplace not only adds to the ambiance, but provides warmth on snowy Ohio winter days.

Kim Korkan and Mary Kay Smith found their own path to the restaurant that was known as The Four Winds some thirty years ago. At first they were guests, but eventually became owners and have been improving the restaurant and their own individual skills ever since, Kim as an accomplished chef and Mary Kay as an effective manager.

In this eclectic town where bead weavers, jewelry designers and artisans of all types sell their wares, Winds has held its own for almost three decades. During that time, Winds was evolving through the counterculture era to finally emerge as a fine dining establishment that promotes a casual "come as you are"

attitude. The term casual elegance best describes the attitude.

It's difficult to describe the menu, because it changes monthly and with each season depending on what produce is available from local farmers. Kim and Mary Kay maintain a loyalty and have cultivated a relationship to local producers of dairy, meats and produce to assure fresh ingredients in their seasonal cuisine and to also support the community.

Generally speaking, the summer menu is abundant in fruits and vegetables and is on the lighter side with salads heaped with newly picked tomatoes, crisp green and white beans, mixed greens and fresh cheese. Fall specialties focus on squash, eggplant, apples and cider ingredients, while the winter menu uses rooted produce that is made into soups and exotic dishes using wild game. Spring brings forth delicacies like tender greens, newly emerged asparagus and fresh herbs. The restaurant provides the best that the earth has to give all year round. Fresh baked breads compliment most any dish and luscious homemade desserts are the perfect ending.

For added balance with any meal the chef recommends a gourmet wine from the restaurant's extensive wine cellar that is adjacent to the restaurant and features specialty wines from all over the world.

Whatever way the wind blows, make sure you breeze in for a seasonal treat.

Address
215 Xenia Ave., Yellow Springs, OH 45387
www.windscafe.com

Phone
(937) 767-1144

Hours
Tuesday - Saturday, 11:30 a.m. – 2:00 p.m.; 5:00 p.m. – 10:00 p.m.

Price Range
$$

Young's Jersey Dairy

"We create fun for our customers by delivering the best customer service, every-day, with the finest in quality products in a clean, safe and entertaining place."

When they say, "come on out to the farm," you can do just that right outside of Yellow Springs. Young's is one of the oldest businesses in Greene County with a history dating back to 1869, when relatives of the Young family built the red barn that still stands today. Over the years many changes have taken place and the business has greatly expanded from a 60-acre farm to a full-fledged ice cream shop that seats about 180, a restaurant that serves home style cooked meals and seats another 180, and an entertainment destination for the entire family. The complex has it all, from the Utters and Putters Miniature Golf course, a driving range and batting cages to a Kiddie Corral and a petting zoo. And the business is still owned and managed by members of the Young family.

Young's Jersey Dairy farm is a step back in time when life was simpler, food was homemade, and ice cream was the main dessert. The Dairy Store is the original ice cream shop, with over 35 flavors (like butter pecan, cookies and cream, white chocolate raspberry swirl, banana, black walnut, cotton candy and bubble gum) served up at any given time, but during the year over a 100 total flavors are available because some flavors are seasonal, like pumpkin and cinnamon in the fall, and peppermint during the Christmas holidays. For those who are watch-

ing their weight and still want a treat there is Gelato and Sorbetto that have less than half the calories and one-third the fat of ice cream, and there are a variety of delicious flavors to choose from. Banana splits and sundaes also top the list and the bakery features homemade favorites like bread pudding, and Schuler's baked donuts, cookies and brownies.

Meals are served in the Golden Jersey Inn, where weekly dinner specials like Pan-fried Cajun Catfish, Oven Baked Tilapia, Grilled Salmon with Pineapple Salsa, and Deep Fried Walleye are featured. Family Value meals include MaMa's Homemade Chicken-n-Dumplins, Grandma's Meatloaf and Buttermilk Chicken. And served daily are Amish Style Beef or Chicken and Noodles, Country Fried Chicken and Taters, Salisbury Steak and Potatoes, and Breaded Pork Tenderloin. A few of the Light and Tasty Selections include Steelhead Trout and Honey Glazed Ham Steak. All are served with a selection of side dishes like green beans, lumpy mashed potatoes, cinnamon spiced apples, homemade steak fries, mac-n-cheese or sweet potato casserole.

This is a real working dairy farm with a large herd of Jersey cattle that are milked daily in the dairy barn and goats that are surrounded by kids (baby goats). In addition, Young's is very involved with the community by sponsoring many events throughout the year (see their event calendar online) as well as hosting hundreds of private parties in the Red Picnic Shelter.

In season, this busy complex welcomes approximately 10,000 visitors per day and in 2001, they clocked approximately 1,350,000 customers who had visited the farm during its history. It's a great place to spend the day with the family — because there is so much to see and do.

DINERS INFORMATION

Address
6880 Springfield Xenia Rd., Yellow Springs, OH 45387
www.youngsdairy.com

Phone
(937) 325-0629

Hours
Sunday - Thursday, 11:00 a.m. – 9:00 p.m.
Saturday - Sunday, 8:00 a.m. – 10:00 p.m.

Price Range
$

CENTRAL EAST
REGION

Adornetto's Italian	Newark, OH
The Boondocks BBQ & Grill	McConnelsville, OH
The Buxton Inn	Granville, OH
Clay Haus	Somerset, OH
The Forum	Cambridge, OH
The Granville Inn	Granville, OH
Longaberger Homestead	Frazeysburg, OH
Main Street Grill & Café	St. Clairsville, OH
Nutcracker Family Restaurant	Pataskala, OH
Popeye's Soda Shop	Dresden, OH
Roots	Lancaster, OH
Shaw's Restaurant & Inn	Lancaster, OH
The Short Story Brasserie	Granville, OH
Tom's Ice Cream Bowl	Zanesville, OH
Vocelli	St. Clairsville, OH
The Warehouse Steak 'n Stein	Coshocton, OH

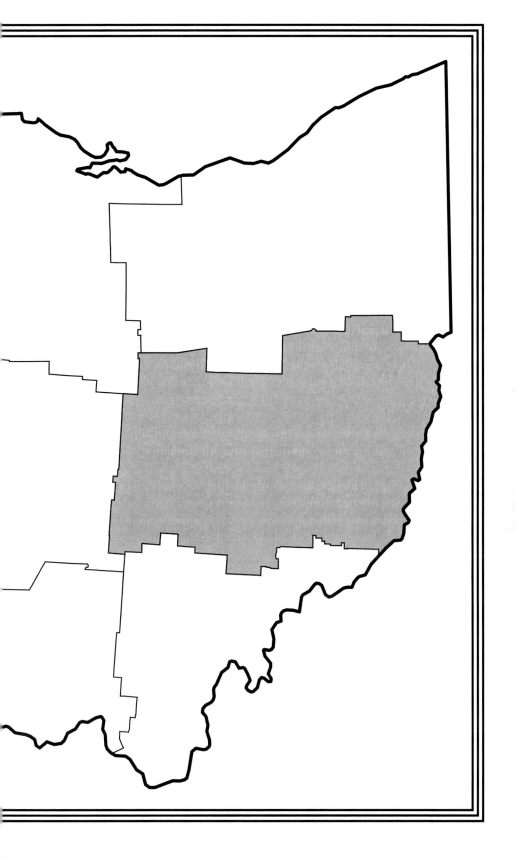

Adornetto's Italian

Newark, OH

ocated behind Walgreens off of 21st Street on the edge of Newark, this attractive restaurant is well known in the area for its pizza, subs and Italian dishes. The focal point in the dining area is a two-story tree growing in the middle of the room right through the ceiling. For safety reasons there is an attractive barricade surrounding it to prevent children who might want to do some climbing after dinner. The stained glass windows brightly depict food and wine, and are particularly beautiful when the sun shines through them. The red brick walls pleasantly contrast with the white oak floors, and the booth seats are made of a colorful woven Italian tapestry.

Family owned, Adornetto's mission statement is that they are "dedicated to being the best dining experience" for its customers. The owner is Mike Sarap. Their fresh pizza dough and hand-made pastas are made daily from

The Pizza People Come Home For

scratch and often bring customers back to enjoy the food in the Tuscan atmosphere.

Their specialties come from two sections of the menu: The Traditional Adornetto's section (Spaghetti and Meatballs, Meat or Four Cheese Raviolo, and Lasagna Al Forno) and the Modern Adornetto's (Fettuccine Alfredo, Penne Carbonaro, and Sausage and Sweet Peppers). No matter what section you choose, the meal will suite your particular taste.

I tried the Tuscan Chicken from the Modern side and found that the marinated chicken strips were exquisitely sautéed with a pinch of garlic and sliced mushrooms, and served over penne pasta covered with homemade Tuscan sauce that is a bit tangy but blends well with the chicken and the pasta. I also had a Mediterranean Salad with mixed greens, artichoke, kalamata, olives, tomatoes and Feta cheese with Mediterranean Dressing, In fact, Adornetto's bottles and sells both their Sweet & Tart Dressing and their House Italian Dressing, so their fine dressings can be enjoyed at home as well.

The main dining room features a luscious ice cream bar where great sundaes are created with Velvet's Original Ice Cream and topped with whipped cream, chocolate, nuts, cherries, butterscotch or whatever you choose.

If you enjoy authentic traditional or modern Italian cuisine, you cannot go wrong at Adornetto's.

CENTRAL EAST

DINERS INFORMATION

Address
250 Goosepond Road, Newark, OH 43055
www.adornettos.com
Check them out on Facebook

Phone
(740) 366-5999

Hours
Monday - Wednesday, 4:00 p.m. – 10:00 p.m.
Thursday, 11:30 a.m. – 10:00 p.m.
Friday - Saturday, 11:30 a.m. – 10:30 p.m.

Price Range
$$

133

The Boondocks BBQ & Grill

McConnelsville, OH

McConnelsville is the county seat of Morgan County located on the eastern side of the Muskingum River with a population under 2000. It is here, on the edge of the river, where I found The Boondocks, that seems appropriately named considering the rural area in which it is located. As I arrived, the owner, Bobby "BJ" Burdette, was warm and welcoming, and I soon learned that he was a graduate of CIA, the world-renowned Culinary Institute of America in New York.

He and his wife, Maria, a certified sous chef from the American Culinary Federation, purchased this establishment in 2007 with the goal of "offering the good folks in Morgan County the same quality eats they would get in the bigger cities, at a price local friends and neighbors could easily afford." The Burdettes vowed from the start to "Keep it simple, keep it good, keep it affordable." And so far they have.

They surveyed the area and determined the type of food that local residents would be interested in and then created a versatile menu with an interesting twist that features appetizers like Pulled Port Quesadillas, Louisiana Crab Cakes and Raider Taters. Signature Sandwiches like The Boondocker (pulled pork piled high on a corn dusted Kaiser roll topped with cole slaw, onion rings and sweet BBQ sauce), Buffalo Chicken (breaded and fried chicken tenders dipped in BJ's award winning Buffalo sauce and topped with Swiss cheese), The Monster Burger (a half pound of fresh never frozen Black

Angus patty with three cheese toppings along with grilled onions, mushrooms, bacon, onion rings, BBQ and Marinara sauces and jalapenos), and hand breaded Southern Fried Catfish Filet. BJ's entrees vary between Hand Cut Ribeye Steak, Butterfly Breaded Shrimp and Chicken Parmesan to Chicken Alfredo Pasta, Baby Back Ribs, and the Surf n' Turf Platter (a ribeye steak and Louisiana crab cakes). All meals are very generous, but the BBQ Combo Platter is for the really hungry guest. It includes a third rack of ribs, a chicken breast, pulled pork, BBQ wings and fried catfish! Wow!

After BJ told me that he had customers that travelled from as far away as Canada, Arizona and Florida, my curiosity was peaked and I was anxious to try some of this award-winning cuisine. I was treated to Mozzarella Skewers that are bite sized cheese cubes battered in tempura, fried in peanut oil and served with a delicious homemade Marinara sauce. The Blue Lump Crab with Cajun ranch seasoning served with crackers was outstanding. It was REAL crab, not the fake stuff. And I also had yummy Buffalo Cheese Fries with mild Buffalo sauce for dipping.

Then there was dessert, all homemade and out of this world. A mouth watering warm Caramel Apple with a sugar glaze just melted in my mouth. And I tried the New York Style Cheesecake served with blueberries, though I had my choice of cherries, hot fudge and pecans. All would have been heavenly.

The good things that are happening at The Boondocks are being noticed nationally. After winning the state BBQ competition in Columbus in 2010, BJ was contacted by the Food Network to be featured on a segment of Diners, Drive-ins and Dives, and, as BJ says, "the rest is history."

DINERS INFORMATION

Address
4653 N. St. Rt. 60, McConnelsville, OH 43756
www.boondocksbbqandgrill.com/splash.asp
www.flavortownUSA.com/boondocks-bbq-and-grill.aspx

Phone
(740) 962-4100

Hours
Monday - Wednesday, 11:00 a.m. – 8:00 p.m.
Thursday - Saturday, 11:00 a.m. – 9:00 p.m.
Sunday, 11:00 a.m. – 6:00 p.m.

Price Range
$$

The
Buxton Inn

Granville, OH

In 1972, Audrey and Orville Orr purchased The Buxton Inn and continued the long tradition of this distinguished establishment. In 2012, they celebrated the landmark's bicentennial, a unique event very few restaurants in American can claim.

Back in 1812, the Inn was built as a comfortable way station at the crossroads of the old stagecoach run serving central Ohio. A remarkably well-restored complex of four structures, there are 25 rooms available that capture the ambiance of a bygone era through primitive antique furnishings.

Just a few short blocks from downtown Granville, the distinctive red buildings with an arched driveway entrance welcome guests. Once inside the main building, there are seven dining areas to choose from all with a unique theme, plus a spacious patio surrounded by colorful, formal flower gardens and relaxing fountains. When I arrived in the middle of the week and around lunch hour, the place was very busy with hungry diners and guests checking in.

Through the years thousands of visitors have made The Buxton Inn their home away from home and have enjoyed the traditional French and American cuisine in the legendary restaurant. One look at either the lunch or dinner menu indicated why. They both offer a variety of delicious and expertly prepared dishes starting with the tangy Cream of Chicken Curry, Dried Cranberry and Toasted Almond Salad served with sharp cheddar cheese and topped with raspberry vinaigrette, and blackened jumbo Cajun Scallops. Entrées, as you would imagine, feature steak, chicken and seafood dishes, but if eating light is a concern there are also pasta dishes, sandwiches and quesadillas on the Lighter Fare menu.

This is definitely fine dining without the high price tag in a relaxed atmosphere, but if you are on a tight budget try one of the reasonably priced early bird specials. Daily specials include a Pasta du Jour entrée with a side salad and dinner rolls. Plus other specials are featured, such as Louisiana Chicken, seasoned and sautéed chunks of chicken breast served with rice and topped with a tasty pimento and mushroom sauce with pieces of artichoke hearts and roasted almonds that I found to be delicious. This is a great place to eat before heading out to explore this delightful town.

DINERS INFORMATION

Address
313 E. Broadway St., Granville, OH 43023
www.buxtoninn.com

Phone
(740) 587-0001

Hours
Tuesday - Saturday, 11:30 a.m. – 2:00 p.m. (lunch); 5:00 p.m. – 9:00 p.m. (dinner)
Sunday, 11:00 a.m. – 3:00 p.m. (brunch); 4:00 p.m. – 8:00 p.m. (dinner)
Tuesday - Thursday, 5:00 p.m. – 6:30 p.m. (Early Bird Specials)

Price Range
$$

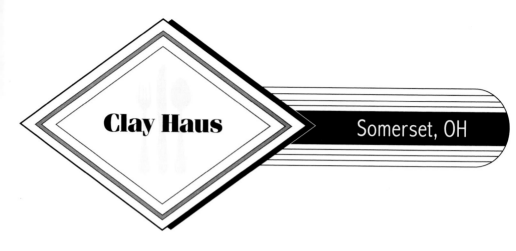

Clay Haus

Somerset, OH

"The past reaching out to the future."

As soon as I set foot on the steps of Clay Haus nestled in the hills of Perry County, I felt like I was being transported back in time. It seemed like deceased owner, Betty Snider (mother of the current owner, Scott, and grandmother to assistant, Chris Riffle), was guiding my thoughts about the historic events that had taken place in this small community. Many prominent figures, like President Andrew Jackson and Henry Clay, had stopped here.

Back in the day, Somerset was a little German village and a rest stop for weary travelers on the Zane Trace Trail (Rt. 22) as they made their way between Zanesville and Lancaster. Built between 1812 and 1820, and modeled after homes in Philadelphia, this structure has seen history transpire first hand. If it only had a voice, it could speak volumes.

A restaurant had existed in this building for many years before the Sniders took over in 1979. They adopted the name Clay Haus for Betty's father Clay and the Pennsylvania Dutch word for house, and continued to serve

the community of Somerset the finest German and American cuisine around. Prior to his becoming owner and manager, Scott had worked with his parents for years and grew to know the ropes both in the kitchen and in the dining room. At this point he is operating the establishment with the help of Chris and together they are doing a fine job.

Scott was an attentive host who had the spirit of hospitality firmly implanted in his character; most likely influenced by Betty. He certainly made me feel welcome in this historic establishment. Of course, it isn't surprising since he grew up in an environment where service to others was important and deeply ingrained. He generously provided me with home cooked favorites of German food and old recipes of early colonial days.

He started off with homemade Bean Dumpling Soup with small semi-button dumplings, which was delicious. Other soups that are available include vegetable, cream chicken and broccoli, tomato bisque and rice as well as cheesy broccoli and potato. The Sauerbraten, which is a marinated roast beef, was laced with sour cream enhanced gravy and very tasty. The Potato Pancakes served with sour cream and applesauce were firm, flavorful and filling. Then there was the Pork Loin with a mild bread dressing. Dark gravy complemented both the dressing and meat very well. A variety of freshly made pies were available including fruit (blueberry, blackberry, apple and cherry) and others (coconut cream, custard and pecan). I had a taste of each and they were delightful and very flavorful. Betty would be proud since she took great pleasure in her pies.

As Betty would say, "Come in, relax, let your mind drift. You may hear the covered wagon stopping at our door to enjoy the best offerings of the comforts of home, and relaxation to the weary traveler!"

CENTRAL EAST

DINERS INFORMATION

Address
123 W. Main Street, Somerset, OH 43783
www.clayhaus.com

Phone
(740) 743-1326

Hours
Tuesday - Thursday, 11:00 a.m. – 8:00 p.m.
Friday - Saturday, 11:00 a.m. – 9:00 p.m.
Sunday, 11:00 a.m. – 3:00 p.m. (Buffet)
Closed between 2-4 p.m. on Tuesday - Saturday

Price Range
$$

The Forum

Cambridge, OH

"Because life is meant to be enjoyed."

Located less than a mile off I-70, The Forum is owned and operated by Alex and Karen Theodosopoulos, whose family has been in the restaurant business for generations. Alex's father, Nick, and grandfather, Gust, immediately entered the food management business when they arrived in America from Greece in 1921 by selling hot dogs on the street.

When we met Alex and Karen, I immediately felt welcomed and at home in The Forum. They were very cordial and shared the story of their remarkable family with us. As the story related to their restaurant, in 1995, Alex and his brother Steve bought a medium-sized eatery off of I-70 known as Tivoli Palace. It was not long before they changed the name to The Forum. Karen remodeled the entire restaurant in less than three weeks and did an excellent job without formal decorating experience. She combined earth tones with stained glass to create a feel for fine dining in a casual atmosphere

Alex is very particular about the quality of the food that he serves to his customers, so he looks for the freshest ingredients that he can find. He also avoids prepackaged items if at all possible and makes desserts, appetiz-

ers, and soups from scratch.

The Forum is where one can find authentic Greek food the likes of which can be found in the Greek Isles. A Greek Sampler includes Spanikopota (a savory spinach pie), Tyropita (three cheeses in a phyllo crust), and Dolmades (stuffed grape leaves) served with fried calamari, feta cheese, Greek olives and Pepperocinis. Saganaki is a sizzling semi-sweet, kasseri cheese dusted with a unique combination of herbs and spices, then pan fried and served in a hot skillet. Excellent!

This was a most enjoyable stop. In Alex's words: "Because life is meant to be enjoyed."

DINERS INFORMATION

Address
2205 Southgate Parkway, Cambridge, OH 43725

Phone
(740) 439-2777

Hours
Sunday - Thursday, 11:00 a.m. – 10:00 p.m.
Friday - Saturday, 11:00 a.m. – 11:00 p.m.
Specialties: Authentic Greek Foods

Price Range
$$

The Granville Inn

Granville, OH

A book about unique and exciting places to eat would not be complete without including the Granville Inn, a landmark listed on the National Register of Historic Places. Warm and welcoming, I felt relaxed as soon as I entered this magnificent Jacobethan Revival style mansion modeled after an English manor. My all night stay was quite comfortable in a modernized room with old world charm. Dinner in the Oak Room before I retired included a vibrant Roasted Carrot and Yellow Pepper Soup with a touch of rosemary cream that complemented the subtle carrot taste, a tender filet of Ohio Raised Beef served with rich béarnaise sauce and mouth watering chive mashed potatoes.

General manager Dena McKinley met with me the next day and gave me a tour of this beautiful and rambling structure that incorporated some of the buildings of the former Granville Female College, which had closed its doors in 1898. The Inn was opened in 1924 in all of its grandeur, complete with hand-cut oak paneling, native sandstone and rural hospitality. The list of distinguished guests is most impressive and the history is much too long to include in this writing, but certainly worth exploring.

Beside the outdoor biergarten where tastings from the extensive wine list are regularly held, I ate lunch on the covered patio and the service was excellent. The menu features fresh and seasonal produce and fine meats along with homemade desserts. The Smoked Salmon and Cream Cheese Tartlet was explosively delicious served with herb vinaigrette and a red onion salad. The rich Classic French Onion Soup Au Gratin was topped with a thick melted gruyere and parmesan cheese which was rich and cheesy. I also had the chunky Chintz Room Chicken Salad, a carry over from the popular dish served in the Chintz Room of the now defunct Lazarus department store café which I remember well. Served on a flaky croissant, it is a great blend of chunks of chicken, whole pecans and bits of celery blended well in a spicy mayonnaise along with fresh fruit on the side. To top off a perfect meal I had the Crème Brulee du Jour. Enough said...I certainly left very satisfied.

Not surprisingly, the Inn has won its share of awards including "Best New Restaurant" by *Columbus Monthly* magazine, the *Wine Spectator* Award of Excellence and one for Columbus' Most Romantic Restaurants.

Address
314 E. Broadway St., Granville, OH 43023
www.granvilleinn.com

Phone
(888) 472-6855

Hours
Hotel: Open 24 Hours
Oak Room: Lunch: Monday - Friday, 11:30 a.m. – 2:00 p.m.
            Dinner: Monday - Thursday, 5:00 p.m. – 9:00 p.m.
                    Friday - Saturday, 5:00 p.m. – 10:00 p.m.
Acorn Pub: Monday - Friday, 4:00 p.m.; Saturday, 2:00 p.m.
Closed Sunday

Price Range
$$$

Longaberger Homestead

Dave Longaberger established his business in 1978, and his trademark baskets have taken the world by storm ever since. When he constructed his multi-complex Longaberger Homestead it was intended to be a "retail, entertainment, and dining complex with a theme of early American crafts-manship." And what is more American than apple pie is a 29-foot tall basket positioned at the entrance gate and filled with huge apples that were being "polished" the day we arrived at the Homestead.

The experience of visiting this unique and incredibly beautiful place will be featured in a future book, but my focus in this book is the restaurants located at the complex. There are three where taste buds can be satisfied during a delightful tour.

The Bakery provides a quick "pick me up" with the choice of Starbucks coffee and other beverages as well as a fresh baked treat or fruit snack.

The Barn BBQ is located in the distinctive white barn where breakfast and lunch are served consisting of generous sandwiches, salads and soups. Box lunches are also available, if ordered ahead, to take with you.

And the Homestead Restaurant is the best place to enjoy a home-cooked meal made from scratch. Though sandwiches and salads are featured, the entrees are worth considering. The Beef or Turkey Pot Roast, Meatloaf, Broasted Chicken and Ham Loaf are all served with a selection of side dishes. The Chicken and Noodles were rich and hardy, and downright delicious.

The décor in the restaurant features many Longaberger products that are used for holding salt and pepper shakers and carrying warm rolls to the dinner table. The shelves along the ceiling will definitely catch your attention with the older "antique" baskets. I was pleasantly surprised to discover that even the silverware had a basket imprinted on it. And I loved eating on the Longaberger plates and bowls because it felt like I was right at home. My mouth watered while watching the homemade desserts delivered to other tables, and had to order their signature dessert labeled "the apple basket," which is a waffle style basket loaded with fresh vanilla ice cream, warm baked apples drizzled with a warm caramel glaze. Yum!

After a good meal, there is nothing more enjoyable than walking along the finely manicured paths surrounded by meticulously detailed landscaping complete with a cast bronze statue of David Longaberger, a reflecting pool and commemorative area dedicated to his memory and accomplishments. It is quite impressive.

This is a great place to visit and enjoy a home cooked meal while shopping for Longaberger baskets.

Address
5563 Raisers Rd., Frazeysburg, OH 43822
www.longaberger.com/homestead/restaurants.aspx

Phone
(740) 322-5588

Hours
June 2 - November 8
Thurdsay, 10:00 a.m. – 5:00 p.m.
Friday - Saturday, 9:00 a.m. – 6:00 p.m.
Sunday, Noon – 5:00 p.m.
Monday - Tuesday, 10:00 a.m. – 5:00 p.m.
Closed Wednesday

Price Range
$$$

145

Main Street Grill & Café

Located in the heart of downtown, this is a classy restaurant which was an unexpected surprise. Not only is it well decorated with beautifully framed pictures, hard wood floors and stained glass windows, but the atmosphere is fresh and clean. Lunch time is pretty casual, but it is strictly black tablecloths for dinner with fresh cut flowers in crystal beaded vases on each table. This is a place with big town elegance without the big town prices. This is also the restaurant that the locals frequent for a good meal whether it is breakfast, lunch or dinner. I always look for spots that local residents enjoy because those are the places that usually offer fine food reasonably priced with good service. And that is exactly what we found at the Main Street Grill and Café.

Owner John Coyne opened Main Street in 2009 and hired Josh Powers as manager and head chef. It is quite obvious that Josh exudes enthusiasm and creativity for his work, because as a trained chef he enjoys creating new

dishes or a new spin on old time favorites.

Josh prepared samples that displayed his skill and ability to combine ingredients for a very tasty result. First up were the Gulf Coast Nachos which is a generous portion of tortilla chips loaded with grilled Old Bay shrimp and real crab meat topped with mozzarella cheese and served with fresh tangy quacamole and chucky salsa. This ranked high on my delicacy scale of good eating. Combining seafood, chips and cheese is a home run in my book. Next up were the Stuffed Mushrooms that were truly good eating. The tender mushrooms were about the size of tennis balls and were filled with an excellent house made fresh claw crab stuffing, minced green pepper, red onions, and, once again, topped with melted mozzarella cheese. Josh received an A+ for this dish. Finally, we tried the Sweet Crab and Shrimp Scampi. Both types of seafood are combined and sautéed in a white wine butter sauce which melds the flavors together and then served over linguini. Absolutely delicious! The menu also features a variety of fish and steak entrees along with tasty desserts.

Though these were more lunch or dinner entrees, breakfast is also available with Eggs and Bacon, Hotcakes, French Toast and Omelets, but there are a few special dishes that you won't get anywhere else, like the Italian Scramble and the Main Street Club.

I am confident that whatever you order here will be delicious. Once again, you get a great meal at a reasonable price. Bon appetite!

CENTRAL EAST

DINERS INFORMATION

Address
110 W. Main Street, St. Clairsville, OH 43950

Phone
(740) 296-5276

Hours
Monday - Friday, 10:00 a.m. – 8:00 p.m.
Saturday, 8:00 a.m. – 8:00 p.m.
Closed Sunday

Price Range
$

Nutcracker Family Restaurant

Pataskala, OH

"Cows may come and cows may go, but the bull in this place goes on forever."

What an unexpected surprise when I walked into this seemingly no frills building and discovered a reminiscent trip back to the 1950s complete with a Rocket gum ball machine at the entrance, a 1948 Band Box Trash Can juke box with Roulette Seeburg speakers mounted on the wall, bags of penny candy, a curvaceous life size car hop, and, of course, hundreds of nutcrackers of all types and sizes.

Originally opened as an ice cream parlor in 1958 in downtown Pataskala, Nancy and Steve Butcher purchased the place in 1995. They eventually moved to Broad Street and expanded their menu, at the same time establishing the 1950s theme. Unfortunately, tragedy struck in 2005 when a devastating fire leveled the building. Steve and Nancy had to rebuild from the ground up, and they optimistically saw it as a chance to design a better floor plan to serve their customers more efficiently. Nancy added the nutcracker idea because it would be a pleasant trademark, and she hoped it would remind her patrons of "Christmas, which is a happy time of year."

It is a great place to grab breakfast or lunch.

The hand-breaded, beer-battered fish sandwich served on a grilled French roll is a big seller, and other popular items include the 8-ounce Texas Tenderloin, the juicy tender quarter pound charbroiled cheeseburger, and the Turkey Sub, or-

dered either hot or cold, which includes a combination of bacon, Swiss and American cheese. And reasonably priced daily Blue Plate Specials include all you can eat fish, clams, spaghetti, chicken, and ham loaf.

There is plenty to choose from for breakfast. Start with the Nutcracker special – two eggs, potatoes, choice of meat all cooked to order plus biscuits and gravy. Ashleigh's Favorite, named after Steve and Nancy's granddaughter, is the most popular item on the breakfast menu. It includes a three egg omelet made with a choice of meat and cheese, along with chopped onions, green peppers, tomatoes, spinach, mushrooms and a side of toast. Home fries are optional. Of course, Sausage Gravy and Biscuits alone make a fine and filling meal. The Banana Nut French Toast sounded delicious especially drenched in warm maple syrup and topped with whipped cream.

Part of the 50s was the luscious desserts, like fruit and cream pies (made fresh daily by Nancy), sundaes of all flavors (chocolate, strawberry, caramel, marshmallow, peanut butter and hot fudge), soda fountain drinks (both cherry and vanilla Coke, and draft root beer in a frosty mug) and an assortment of floats.

To make your meal more affordable, kids eat free on Tuesdays, loyalty cards are available that give a discount on future meals, and veterans eat free twice a year around Veterans Day and Memorial Day.

There is something for everyone here surrounded by a fun and upbeat atmosphere at a reasonable price. On the way out, buy a bag of rich Amish chocolates for the road.

DINERS INFORMATION

Address
63 E. Broad St., Pataskala, OH 43062
www.nutcrackerpataskala.com

Phone
(740) 964-0056

Hours
Sunday - Monday, 7:00 a.m. – 2:00 p.m.
Tuesday - Saturday, 7:00 a.m. – 8:00 p.m.
Specalties: Candy Shop, Amish chocolates, nuts, homemade pies, soda shop

Price Range
$

Popeye's Soda Shop

Dresden, OH

This is a fun place located in the heart of downtown Dresden not far from the Longaberger Homestead. The Soda Shop was opened by Dave Longaberger in 1963 for $135 when he was moving into the restaurant business. It was known as the Midway Dairy Bar at the time, but the nickname that Dave gave it eventually stuck and it was renamed Popeye's Soda Shop.

Patterned after the ever-popular 1950s soda shop, the décor is authentic with metal chairs and red plastic seats. The old jukebox, the stand alone and the tabletop versions, really got a work out when the teens invaded the soda shop and popped their nickels in for one song. It was a bargain to get six for quarter. The menu at Popeye's is similar to what was served during that era with the Chili Cheese Dogs, Grilled Bologna, and Fries in a Basket. Popeye's Original (a generous order of thinly sliced ham stacked on a Kaiser roll and served with a cup of Bean soup) is what those in my hometown of Pittsburgh called chipped or chopped ham. The milkshakes back then were made with real, whole milk, Hershey's chocolate whipped up in a professional blender and poured out of the stainless steel blender cup into a tall shake glass. Then

it was topped with real whipped cream. That is how Popeye's serves it today.

Hamburgers and cheeseburgers were what we ate before there was a fast food drive thru on every corner. We had to walk into the restaurant and sit down to eat.

The Wimpy Burger served at Popeye's is reminiscent of the burger from yesteryear. Two juicy hamburger patties smothered in Popeye's special sauce with melted American cheese served with lettuce, tomato, pickles and onion. Now that is a burger! I can hear Wimpy saying, "I would kindly pay you Tuesday for a Hamburger today!"

However, there are items on the menu that would have been unimaginable back in the day. The Buffalo Chicken Wrap would conjure images of Buffalos wrapping themselves up on the plains. The Chicken Finger Basket would also beg the question, "Do chickens really have fingers?" Sweet Potato Fries would have been another oddity in that sweet potatoes are what we eat at Thanksgiving.

So we have made some great improvements over the past 60-something years. At the same time, we have left behind a legacy for future generations and I have to wonder if Popeye's can show those generations what it was like to live in the 50s. So far, they are giving it a good try.

DINERS INFORMATION

Address

415 Main St., Dresden, OH 43821

www.longaberger.com/resources/6/homestead/Popeyes%20Soda%20
    Shop%20Menu.pdf

Phone

(740) 754-5730

Hours

Monday - Thursday, 11:00 a.m. – 5:00 p.m.
Friday - Saturday, 11:00 a.m. – 6:00 p.m.
Sunday, Noon – 5:00 p.m.

Price Range

$

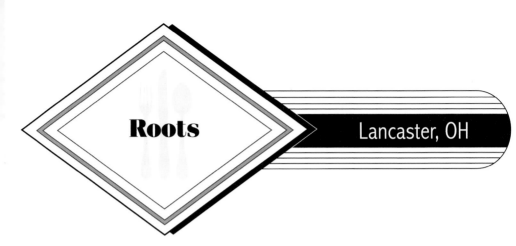

Roots — Lancaster, OH

Lancaster was a much different town back in 1950 when Merle and Eloise Root moved into a modest house on a small road known as Memorial Drive. When they decided to get into the food business, they transformed their home into a restaurant to serve the local people. This restaurant became Roots. It was not only their family surname, but also a place guests could call home and put down their "roots." Eventually, Jeff and Janet Graf purchased the restaurant and their son, Chris Straum, helps manage the business. He was also a wealth of history and information when I visited.

I asked guest Vern Miller why he came to Roots, and he said he had been eating at this hometown establishment for more than 50 years, ever since his days as a lineman with the South Central Power Company where he retired 20 years ago. He added that his roots were certainly sunk in Roots. Irving and Shirley Small said that they would not pass up a trip to the place on their frequent visits to Lancaster.

This homey restaurant where many guests simply ask for "the usual," has that warm familiar feeling that I always felt when I walked into my grandmother's kitchen. Great aromas drifted in the air that immediately stirred my appetite. Daily specials have been a part of the lineup for years and have not changed much. Char-broiled Chicken, English Pot Roast, Chicken Stir Fry, and Salmon Patties are staples, but there is also a 16-oz T-bone, a 10 oz. lean cut char-

broiled New York Strip Steak and even an 8-oz. Prime Rib. A variety of seafood dishes are bound to satisfy the desire for a treat from the ocean or a nearby lake. Freshly breaded, deep-fried perch or catfish filets give the customer the option of choosing a sandwich or served plain with tartar sauce. And the jumbo fantail shrimp, fishtail and the salmon patty dinners come with two sides. A choice of homemade mashed potatoes and gravy, green beans, pickled beets, creamed pea salad, broccoli cauliflower salad, cole slaw or a cup of cheesy cream of broccoli soup compliment most any meal. The heavenly aromas wafting in the air are the result of freshly baked pies (cherry, rhubarb, Dutch apple and butterscotch), but there is a variety of cream, lemon and coconut pies, too.

The homemade broccoli soup was thick and tasty, with big chunks of broccoli. And the baked chicken breast was tender and moist, easy to cut with a fork, and served with mashed potatoes and gravy. It was a meal that took me back to my roots in Pennsylvania. To finish off a perfect meal, I had a piece of coconut cream pie, which just hit the spot. The meringue was firm, brownish peaks and the cream was peppered with slivers of coconut. Delicious!

Of the 14 restaurants on North Memorial Drive within a two-mile stretch, Roots is one of the best Mom and Pop spots for good food and friendly atmosphere.

DINERS INFORMATION

Address
1260 N. Memorial Dr., Lancaster, OH 43130
Check them out on Facebook

Phone
(740) 653-8944

Hours
Monday - Saturday, 6:00 a.m. – 8:00 p.m.
Sunday, 8:00 a.m. – 4:00 p.m.

Price Range
$

Shaw's Restaurant & Inn

Lancaster, OH

Shaw's restaurant, located at Broad and Chestnut, was originally opened by Harry Shaw in 1947 and sold to Bruce and Jean Cork in 1975. Shaw also owned the Lancaster Hotel located at 123 Broad Street and upon his death, the Corks purchased the hotel and relocated the restaurant to the Broad Street location, thus combining it with the hotel. After the main and lower floors were renovated in 1989, the current name of Shaw's Restaurant and Inn was adopted. The building is unique for Lancaster, constructed in 1941 with six stories and 25 suites, all of which have a different décor.

The restaurant, which features American cuisine with an emphasis on aged in-house steaks, is one of the finest in the area. Under the direction of general manager Susie Cork, the daughter of Bruce and Nancy, many innovative and creative programs have emerged. She began the Cooking Studio that regularly features classes taught by Susie, a graduate of The Culinary School at Kendall College in Chicago. Other special events sponsored by

the restaurant are live music, wine and beer tastings, and a Beer, Barbeque and Blue Grass Festival. Shaw's is also very involved in the annual Lancaster Festival that provides a variety of entertainment throughout the week and in many areas of the community.

The menu is changed quarterly to appeal to younger diners, and seasonal items like lobster is featured during specific months. Specialty dishes feature hand cut steaks, soft shell crab, and fresh Walleye and Lake Erie perch. All desserts are homemade from scratch, as are salad dressings, and only the freshest ingredients are used which are often purchased from local growers. Being ever conscious of their customers needs, special menus are available for those with allergies or gluten sensitivity.

I have been going to Shaw's for almost 30 years and have never had anything but great meals and the best service. This is a restaurant that has remained consistent throughout the years, which is the mark of a truly fine restaurant.

DINERS INFORMATION

Address
123 North Broad St., Lancaster, OH 43130
www.shawsinn.com

Phone
(800) 654-2477

Hours
Monday - Saturday, 7:00 a.m. – 9:00 p.m.
Sunday, 7:00 a.m. – 8:00 p.m.

Price Range
$$

The Short Story Brasserie

Don't be put off by the name for in French, according to Miriam Webster, a brasserie is a "type of restaurant with a relaxed, upscale setting, which serves single dishes and other meals." This lovely, out of the way spot located on the edge of Granville bears a literature theme, which is quite evident by the Key West posters and the portrait of the owner James Housteau's favorite writer. The menu is creatively designed like a book with three parts (Chilled Small Plates, Hot Small Plates and Large Plates) along with a Denouement (in literary terms, the events that take place after the literary element known as the climax of a narrative) and finally the Footnotes. Each of these references feature dishes that include a dramatic and satisfying experience.

From Part I, I sampled the Baby Arugula Salad with roasted pepper, brioche and goat cheese, which was fresh and crispy clearly preparing my palate for Part II. The Quick Fire Lobster Thermidor is a creamy pot pie with a rich mixture of lobster and scallops accented with chopped onions and sliced mushrooms. It is absolutely delicious. Mr. Housteau then recommended the lamb belly that admittedly made me nervous and reminded me of some of the weird food that the television restaurant reviewers eat, but my apprehension turned to anticipation when I learned that this was really lamb breast. I found it to be tender and juicy,

THE SHORT STORY
Brasserie

nothing like I imagined, and served with roasted garlic and hummus that complimented the sweetness of the lamb. Part III was the Macaroni and Cheese, which was nothing like what I make at home. It was laced with chunks of lobster and served in a French black truffle and, once again, a tasty surprise. Another surprise was Chef Robert's Crab Cake with saffron whole grain mustard aioli, which is a sauce combining olive oil, crushed garlic, egg yolks and lemon juice, just perfect for the crab cakes that are often dry. I finished this tasting experience with a light and fluffy Warm Chocolate Souffle that certainly warmed my soul.

The combined experience of Mr. Housteau, who has a French background, and his chef, Robert Harrison, who was trained at the renowned Culinary Institute of America in New York, has created a most unique restaurant. Its casual elegance provides a relaxed atmosphere where the weary traveler can enjoy an excellent meal and an exquisite glass of imported wine.

Mr. Housteau told me that as a young boy his father taught him how to work hard and his mother taught him how to dream big. In his world travels, he has developed a zest for diverse cuisine as well as an extensive knowledge of international wines that is the backbone of his restaurant. Owning The Short Story Brassiere truly fulfills his dreams.

DINERS INFORMATION

Address
923 River Road, Granville, OH 43023
www.theshortstoryrestaurant.com

Phone
(740) 587-0281

Hours
Sunday - Thursday, 5:00 p.m. – 8:00 p.m.
Friday - Saturday, 5:00 p.m. – 10:00 p.m.
Sunday Brunch, 9:00 a.m. – 2:00 p.m.
Reservations strongly recommended

Price Range
$$$

Tom's Ice Cream Bowl

Zanesville, OH

Who doesn't like ice cream? Reputedly one of the best places to get almost any flavor you like is at Tom's Ice Cream Bowl in Zanesville. Located near the historic Y-Bridge, this is a definite stop to satisfy any sweet tooth. Tom's also features old-fashioned, hand dipped milkshakes and almost any other type of confection treat you can think of, along with sandwiches and drinks. All the ice cream is handmade in a wide variety of seasonal flavors, like watermelon during the summer, pumpkin in the fall, and peppermint around the holidays.

We enjoyed a sundae while talking with owner Bill Sullivan, who shared the story of how he became involved in the ice cream business. While we spoke, the place was a buzz with people coming and going with their sweet treats or enjoying conversation over dinner.

In 1948, with only four tables and a counter seating for seven, the doors to Tom's first location opened. In 1953, Tom's moved to the new location

on McIntire Avenue. On April 1, 1984, Tom retired at the age of 69 and sold Tom's Ice Cream Bowl to Bill Sullivan, his former manager. Since that day, Bill has pledged to maintain the fine quality and excellent service created by Tom un-

til the day he retires. That may be some time in the distant future, since he loves the business and enjoys talking with and meeting new customers. Bill worked at Tom's during his high school years and after a brief leave of absence returned as manager and eventually owner. Since taking over, he has experimented with many different flavors in order to keep the customers returning.

Tom's has been an icon in Zanesville and has been recognized in many articles that have appeared in national publications like *USA Today*, which listed Tom's as one of the "10 Great Places in America to Get a Scoop." It was also listed in "The Best of Country" in *Country Living Magazine* as one of the best roadside eats for sweet treats. *Ohio Magazine* also mentions Tom's regularly as one of Ohio's Best Ice Cream locations in the state.

Stop in today and taste some local history for yourself and some darn good ice cream!

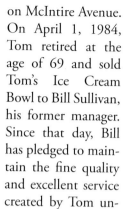

CENTRAL EAST

DINERS INFORMATION

Address
532 McIntire Ave., Zanesville, OH 43701
www.tomsicecreambowl.com

Phone
(740) 452-5267

Hours
Tuesday - Thursday, 11:00 a.m. – 10:00 p.m.
Friday - Saturday, 11:00 a.m. – 11:00 p.m.
Sunday, 11:00 a.m. – 10:00 p.m.

Price Range
$

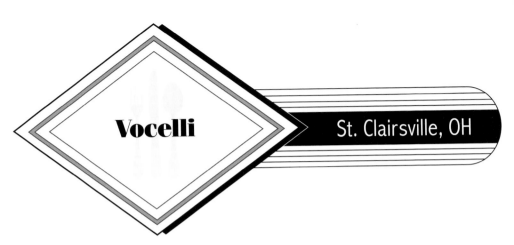

Vocelli

St. Clairsville, OH

There are thousands of pizza places across America, and we not only enjoy the convenience, but also find comfort in a good pizza. We also have our favorites that depend considerably on the type of topping and crust thickness. St. Clairsville is no different than any other town, but we were able to find a pizza place with a twist – Gourmet Pizza. Now how does a gourmet pizza differ from the everyday variety?

Some of the gourmet toppings offered are Chicken Alfredo Spinach, which is very tasty with a ranch sauce, also Buffalo Chicken (chicken strips drenched in Buffalo sauce and topped with a mozzarella cheese on creamy ranch sauce), Steakhouse Ranch (tender steak, red onions and mozzarella cheese and again on ranch sauce), Meat Magnifico (pepperoni, ham, capicola, fresh bacon, savory Italian sausage and mozzarella), and the Hawaiian (sweet pineapple, ham, crisp bacon on the traditional tomato pizza sauce and topped with a generous amount of mozzarella cheese). These are just a few of the many selections from which to choose.

In addition, there are gourmet salads that are served in a pizza crust and include the Antipasta, the Mediterranean, the Tuscan Grilled Chicken and Chicken Caesar. The variety of appetizers is a great way to warm up to the experience of a gourmet pizza. Bruschetta, Cheesesticks, Chicken Tenders Italiano, and Garlic Bread can feed a crowd. Vocellis is also known for their Strombolias as well as their Gourmet Subs.

And in keeping with the rest of the gourmet fare, finish the meal off with a delectable dessert; choose between Tiramisu, Chocolate Fudge Layer Cake or Connoli.

Not only is Vocellis a carry out, but they also deliver to eleven local hotels, which is a great benefit for anyone staying in the area and arriving dog tired after a long drive. Taking the kids to a local restaurant may be too overwhelming, so just order in. Most motels don't have room service and many don't have a place to eat on the premises. So this is a perfect solution. Vocellis even provides coupons to make your meal more affordable for families and individuals alike, so look for them in the travel books and other publications.

DINERS INFORMATION

Address
165 W. Main St., St. Clairsville, OH 43950
www.vocellipizza.com

Phone
(740) 695-4005

Hours
Monday - Thursday, 10:00 a.m. – 11:00 p.m.
Friday, 10:00 a.m. – Midnight
Saturday, 11:00 a.m. – Midnight
Sunday, 11:00 a.m. – 11:00 p.m.

Price Range
$$

After more than 30 years as an educator, John Larsen turned his sights toward being an entrepreneur and purchased The Warehouse Steak n' Stein located in historic Roscoe Village. Housed in an old warehouse that was built in 1831, it is only one of many buildings in the Village that hale their roots back to the days when the Ohio and Erie Canal was just being established. The Canal transported people and goods from Lake Erie and the Ohio River, and the warehouse was used to store these goods — grain, hides, wool and produce — that were sold to residents in area towns and villages. This was a popular place back then, and it is a popular place some 180 years later. Restored and updated, The Warehouse provides a gathering place in a relaxed setting with live music and expertly prepared food.

John's inspiration came from his father, Oscar, and uncle, Ray (Bud) Arnold, who were partners in a tavern known as "Fred and Harold's" in Zanesville. Eventually, they turned it into The Steak n' Stein and the Arnold family operated it until 1999. John's cousin, Amy Arnold, is now the manager of The Warehouse with other family members working in the business too.

John has done an excellent job of converting this immense building into useable space. The three finished floors and an expansive patio all have their own atmosphere. The Comedy Club, dining room, tavern, banquet room, and patio have a different focus, but they all have one goal in common and that is to make guests feel at home. The staff works hard to keep up with the steady

stream of orders, but they are still attentive to the patrons' needs and delivered food and drinks promptly. Whether indoors or outside on the patio, weather permitting, the live music adds to the relaxed setting.

The Warehouse is known for its Pin-

wheel Steak topped with Stein Rings, the 10 oz. Porterhouse Pork Chop, seasoned and pan seared Great Lakes Walleye and Lemon-Pepper Chicken Breast. Many variations of the Flatbread Pizza are available for a quick meal as are a whole range of sandwiches, from the P.R. Nye's Cheeseburger and Deep Fried or Grilled Pork Tenderloin to the Canal Club ("not your traditional club") and even Ham-Garlic Bologna.

John buys locally raised beef and is particular when it comes to the quality of food that comes out of the kitchen, and always works with the chef to develop new items they can add to the menu.

When asked whether he enjoys owning a restaurant after a long and unrelated career, John said, "You find a job that you love and you add five days to your weekend." Enough said!

DINERS INFORMATION

Address
400 N. Whitewoman Street, Roscoe Village, Coshocton, OH 43812
www.warehousesteaknstein.com

Phone
(740) 622-4001

Hours
Kitchen Hours (hours may vary during winter months)
Monday - Thursday, 11:00 a.m. – 10:00 p.m.
Friday - Saturday, 11:00 a.m. – 11:00 p.m.
Sunday, 11:00 a.m. – 8:00 p.m.

Price Range
$$

SOUTH WEST
REGION

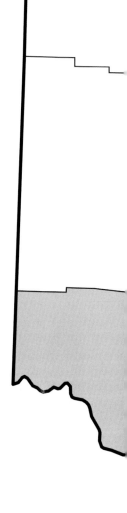

45 East	Oxford, OH
Bacall's Café	Cincinnati, OH
Bangkok Palace	Chillicothe, OH
Beaugard's Southern Bar "B" Que	Wilmington, OH
Cruiser's Diner	Seaman, OH
The Dock at Water	Chillicothe, OH
Firehouse Grill	Cincinnati, OH
The General Denver Hotel	Wilmington, OH
The Golden Lamb Restaurant and Inn	Lebanon, OH
La Cascada	Hillsboro, OH
Lake White Club	Waverly, OH
Los Mariachis	Chillicothe, OH
Moyer Winery and Restaurant	Manchester, OH
Murphin Ridge Inn	West Union, OH
Old Canal Smoke House	Chillicothe, OH
The Old Y Restaurant	Winchester, OH
The Portsmouth Brewing Company	Portsmouth, OH
The Scioto Ribber	Portsmouth, OH
Spillway Lodge	Clarksville, OH

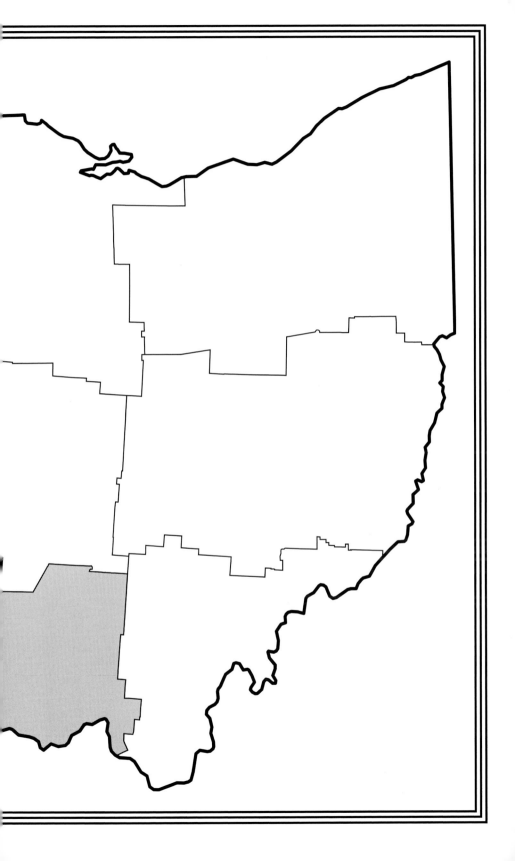

45 East

Oxford, OH

Oxford is the home of Miami University (M.U.), with its beautiful sprawling campus only blocks from downtown, and High Street is the main drag through town. Typical of most college towns, there are many restaurants, bars, and grills. However, 45 East has withstood the test of time by staying in business despite many challenges. One challenge was a fire in the 1980s that took out the entire block, destroying everything in its path. The restaurant closed at that time for repairs, but eventually reopened and has been operating ever since.

I met with manager Jeremiah Robuck, a 2000 graduate of M.U., who had left town and worked for a while but returned in order to work for 45 East. He gave us a tour of the facility and filled us in on the most popular food items.

He pointed out that the signature dishes are suggested by the employees, for the most part, because they hear the patrons' comments and follow through with special requests. A few of the items that have become popular as a result are the hand cut French dip Prime Rib and the Philly Cheese Steak sandwiches. The Gourmet Sub (combination of turkey, salami, pepperoni and cheese) and the spicy Salmon Sandwich (a hand pattied salmon croquet on toasted foccaccia herb bread with chardonnay sauce) are also big sellers. The House Pasta cannot be ignored and consists of marinated grilled chicken breast and sautéed Tiger shrimp tossed with penne rigate and the house signature tomato vodka cream sauce. The Broasted Fried Chicken completes the general category of dishes available but is far from all the entrees that they offer. It's worth checking out their web site to see some of the other items.

They also have a sushi bar by the name of Tonic Sushi Bar & Lounge that is separate from 45, but in the same building where an extensive selection of favorite sushi items are offered on its own menu. These two restaurants are related but different, if you know what I mean. However, both serve fine quality food and they take great pride in serving college students, their families (children are welcome and they have their own menu), or just hungry travelers passing through town.

DINERS INFORMATION

Address
45 East High St., Oxford, OH 45056
www.45eastbarandgrill.com

Phone
(513) 523-3737

Hours
Monday - Saturday, 11:00 a.m. – 2:30 a.m.
Sunday, 11:00 a.m. – 10:00 p.m.

Price Range
$

Bacall's Café

Cincinnati, OH

Bacall's is not a white tablecloth kind of place, but it is upscale and they serve excellent, reasonably priced meals in a relaxed and comfortable setting. Located on busy Hamilton Rd. in Cincinnati, it has an easily recognizable glass block entrance and features creative Art Deco décor throughout. Limited parking is available on the street though there is a parking lot across the street from the restaurant.

Seating in the bar area provides a sports atmosphere complete with two televisions, but on the other side of the divider is where the roar of the sports crowd ceases. The dining room is more private and quaint and most of the time Sally will be serving as she has for more than 20 years. She knows her usual customers like family, and a new patron may be put off by the kidding

and teasing that goes on, but it just lends an air of familiarity that goes with the territory. The menu is well-balanced with a large selection of homemade favorites. There are Starters (Artichoke Spinach dip, Blackened Chicken Quesadilla, Southwestern Spring Rolls), Lite Bites (soup and sandwich specials), Soups (Wisconsin Cheddar, Chili and a daily special), Salads (from Grilled Chicken and the Chef Salad to Tuna Plate and Danny's Salad), Bit-o-Salads ("same great salads but a bit smaller in portion and cost"), Sandwiches (Jack Salmon, Reubens, Open Face Roast Beef and Cincy Hot Brown), Burgers (Black and Bleu, Burger Bacon Dog and Southwest Spicy), and finally the Entrees (Chicken Parmesan, Beer Battered Cod, N.Y. Strip and the Catch of the Day) with a variety of sides.

I had the Wisconsin Cheese Soup, which was very thick and cheesy. The Artichoke dip was a little different in that the spinach, green chilis and artichokes were chopped, but all was blended well with mayo, which made it perfect for eating with chips or even a spoon.

No matter what you're looking for, you will find something that satisfies your taste. And remember to say, "Hi" to Sally for me.

DINERS INFORMATION

Address
6118 Hamilton Ave., Cincinnati, OH 45224
www.bacallscafe.com

Phone
(513) 541-8804

Hours
Monday - Thursday, 11:00 a.m. – 11:00 p.m.
Friday - Saturday, 11:00 a.m. – Midnight
Sunday, 4:00 p.m. – 10:00 p.m.

Price Range
$$

SOUTH WEST

Bangkok Palace

More than two decades ago, Chai and Kristina Jauruwanakorn purchased this restaurant in the busy shopping area north of Chillicothe. In the meantime, major chain stores have sprung up around Bangkok Palace, but this excellent restaurant has prevailed. As one of the most popular shopping hubs in the south central region of the state, the traffic on Bridge Street is quite heavy, and shoppers are always looking for a good sit down meal. They certainly will find it here. My husband John and I have enjoyed their cuisine since they opened and have never been disappointed. There is not only a wide variety of entrees to choose from, but the staff has always been attentive and considerate. The prices are very reasonable, the location is convenient, and there is plenty of parking.

Many members of the family are involved in some aspect of the business including Chai's brother, Kitticitai, and nephew Niwai, who share the cooking and kitchen duties with Chai. Though busy raising their four children, Kristina has always helped in the dining room along with a sister-in-law Ampai.

The extensive menu offers a full complement of delicacies from hot appetizers, sushi and soups to the Chef's Suggestions and entrees. The most popular entrée and the one John always orders is Pad Thai, which is a spicy hot dish for those who need a little kick. The Thai noodle is seasoned with egg, chili powder, scallions, bean sprouts and minced shrimp and will surely raise

your temperature though the chef will tone it down by special request. My favorite dish is the Triple Crown that is a tasty combination of crab, shrimp and scallops blended in a lobster sauce with crispy Chinese vegetables served over rice (steamed or fried). Moo Goo Gai Pan is also popular and is a breast of chicken sautéed with assorted vegetables, also served with rice. Another favorite, Thai Curry Chicken is seasoned with Thai spices and cooked in a rich curry base with coconut milk to offset the spiciness of the chicken that is not only very tasty but healthy as well.

There are many other selections, but overall the food is consistently delicious, well prepared and delivered promptly. Most items are ala carte but the portions are generous and there is usually enough to take home for a snack later. The restaurant is clean and comfortable, and the abundance of windows provide plenty of light and a nice view of the area. No matter what you order, you'll enjoy your visit to Bangkok Palace.

DINERS INFORMATION

Address
8970 N. Bridge St., Chillicothe, OH 45601

Phone
(740) 773-8424

Hours
Monday - Thursday, 11:00 a.m. – 9:00 p.m.
Friday, 11:00 a.m. – 10:00 p.m.
Saturday, Noon – 10:00 p.m.
Sunday, Noon – 8:00 p.m.

Price Range
$

Beaugard's Southern Bar "B" Que

After 22 years in the Air Force, Marty Beaugard moved back home and took over the family business from his parents who had operated the restaurant since 2000, but had more than 40 years experience in food service. He has been working in this converted fast food structure ever since. Located in a shopping center on the north side of Wilmington, I was particularly impressed at how clean this restaurant was, so much so I felt that I could literally eat off the floor. The old fashioned steel framed chairs with the red padded seats were quite comfortable and the atmosphere was pleasant. As I looked around I found the hog décor everywhere from the cute hog border on the walls to the giant hog standing guard by the counter as an official greeter to guests.

In keeping with the southern tradition of his parents, Marty smokes all the meat until it has acquired a juicy, tender perfection. Spare ribs, brisket, and pulled pork are served with a generous helping of his homemade BBQ sauce in three strengths — mild, medium and hot — that is cooked in a smokehouse behind the restaurant for hours. The rich mild sauce is the perfect compliment for the hardy flavor of his pork dishes. Marty trims his brisket leaving a thin layer of fat to add taste and then cooks it for about four hours to give it the tender texture that allows it to be cut with a fork. The menu features the half-pound or one pound of pulled brisket along with two sides, like BBQ beans, macaroni salad or mac and cheese. Sandwiches are served on a toasted bun with a side order of homemade sandwich slaw, which is a cabbage side dish made with vinegar and sugar instead of mayonnaise. If pork is not what you are looking for, the menu also offers chicken as well as the Big Beau Burger that comes in two sizes — quarter pound and half pound. You can also treat yourself to a deep fried catfish or cod sandwich or even fried bologna topped with mayo, mustard or, what else, BBQ sauce.

A taste of southern hospitality is evident in the freshly brewed sweet tea and the friendliness of the servers, but what makes this a special place is Marty's outgoing personality and his personal attention to preparing barbeque sauce. It is not surprising that Beaugard's was chosen by the *Cincinnati Enquirer* as the "Best Real Southern Barbeque."

Cruiser's Diner

Seaman, OH

A visit to this stainless steel rocket diner is like a quick trip back to the 1950s, when life was simpler and food was reasonably priced. The casual atmosphere is inviting for the entire family, and the restaurant serves American food that appeals to guests of all ages, like meatloaf, ½ pound burgers, roast beef, chicken sandwiches, deep fried pickles, and chili cheese fries.

Shipped in two pieces from Florida in the late 1990s, the diner was erected along the main highway of St. Rt. 32 that runs between Cincinnati and Athens. To draw the attention of passers by, owners Steve Cacaro and Barry McFarland chose to trim the exterior with red neon string lights. Once inside the door, the décor of bright lights, checkered floor, red vinyl and silver metal chairs, and the spacious booths reminded me of a set from the Happy Days television show. From the metal counter, guests can view the delectable

desserts in the glass display case. From my booth, I gazed at the walls filled with 1950s paraphernalia – LP record covers, celebrity pictures and models of cars from yesteryear, signs advertising Mountain Dew, Fire Chief Tobacco, Kayo Chocolate Drink and Route 66 which enhanced the decor.

The restaurant not only attracts tourists, but locals who are looking for good old-fashioned meals for breakfast, lunch and dinner. Daily specials like hot ham and cheese, beef and noodles, lasagna, salmon patties, baked steak and soups add variety for regulars who frequent the diner. Take out service is also available. The cod sandwiches are deep fried and never frozen, and the meatloaf is moist and filling. I finished the meal with a heaping piece of coconut cream pie that just hit the spot.

The full menu is served all day, and the portions are worth the price. Leann, the general manager, and Kayla were friendly and efficient, and made my visit very enjoyable. True to its name, Cruisers sponsors a "Cruise In" during May where cars from the region and beyond drive in. If you are in the area, drop by and relive the 1950s.

DINERS INFORMATION

Address
155 Stern Drive, Seaman, OH 45679
Phone
(937) 386-3330
Hours
Sunday - Thursday, 7:30 a.m. – 9:00 p.m.
Friday - Saturday, 7:30 a.m. – 10:00 p.m.
Price Range
$

SOUTH WEST

The Dock at Water

Chillicothe, OH

I n the heart of downtown Chillicothe, the Dock at Water is the local watering hole that attracts visitors and residents alike. It's a great place to meet up with old friends, celebrate a special occasion or just have a relaxed, laid back lunch or dinner in the spacious dining area or on the covered patio. Music is always playing whether it is live or piped in, which lifts the spirits after a long day. This is one of the most popular gathering places in the area.

The food is down to earth and will satisfy every taste starting with the appetizers of Fried Veggies with Ranch dressing for dipping, the Dock Fries dripping with cheese and bacon, Chicken Chunks and Chicken Wings. Can't make up your mind, then order the Water Street Whale which is a sample of four items: Peppered Chicken, Chicken Tenders, Mini Burgers and Cheese

Sticks. A variety of salads (Chicken Bite Delight, Grilled or BBQ Chicken Salad, Taco, and Black and Blue) can be served alone or with the soup of the day. You can substitute the soup for a sandwich, wrap or fajita. Hanner's Home Run (breaded or grilled tenderloin) is named after a local celebrity, Dr. Chris Hanners, who owns the Chillicothe Paints minor league baseball team. Then, of course, there is a selection of burgers, pizza and pasta dishes. But if you are serious about having a good meal, choose one of their steaks (rib-eye, strip or sirloin) or Char-Grilled Prime Rib.

This sports bar has changed ownership many times over the years. At one time it was a teen nightclub called Mariah's that was alcohol free, but as The Dock it has one of the longest bars in the area where one can find a wide selection of beer, wine and spirits. Generous seating abounds and when filled to capacity it can accommodate about 225 patrons. Whether you sit at one of the high top tables or in one of the many intimate booths, you always have a good view of the ten televisions that hang high in the air and adorn the place.

You can always get a good meal and beverage or two at a reasonable price that fits any budget. I'm always pleasantly surprised when I receive my check at the end of the evening knowing that I didn't break the bank.

DINERS INFORMATION

Address
80 E. Water Street, Chillicothe, OH 45601

Phone
(740) 779-3625

Hours
Daily, 11:00 a.m. — closing varies

Price Range
$

Firehouse Grill

Cincinnati, OH

Located in the spacious suburbs of Cincinnati, The Firehouse Grill is a unique restaurant sitting on a large corner lot surrounded by the beauty of nature on all sides. According to owner and former firefighter, Bob Davis, The Firehouse Grill began with a mental spark. He had the desire to revive the memories of good times and good food he had experienced years ago at a previous restaurant in the same locale. He remembered that what made this location successful were the unparalleled views from the patio, lunch hour wraps, private meeting space, and live music. This inspired him to resurrect his old hang out and to accentuate the things that made it great. He replaced the old bar with a new 36 seat bar that is a perfect place to see one of the suspended televisions. He upgraded the patio to outshine its former glory and now offers outdoor dining with a view of the lake. The old crowd began to return and, much to Bob's delight, they are bringing their friends. It's starting to look like the old place he had once known.

When we walked through the large heavy doors, we were taken back at the immensity of the place. It is 12,000 square feet under roof with 25 ft. beamed ceilings and a wood and brick interior. Despite its size, we found a corner in the large dining room where we were able to have a private conversation with the execu-
tive chef, Jason.
The spacious pri-
vate party room
is complete with
a 55" flat screen
TV and can be
booked for most
any private event.
There is seating
for 380 diners
inside the restau-

rant and room for another 180 on the patio.

Jason filled us in on some of the popular specials that included Buffalo Chicken Rolls, Baked Pretzel Sticks, Shrimp Carbonara, Sure Fire Pizza and the Classic Caesar Salad. He gave us a little insight about The Black Fire Wrap, which contains blackened chicken, caramelized onion, chipotle mayonnaise, Monterey jack, and shredded lettuce, all wrapped in a jalapeno cheddar tortilla. The Back Draft Burger is ground sirloin topped with jalapenos, chilis, melted Monterey Jack, guacamole and bacon. The Engine House Tilapia is tortilla crusted and served atop jalapeno corn pudding, black bean salsa and guacamole. He also serves a tender, hand cut New York Strip Steak as well as his form of surf and turf, which is simply called Steak and Shrimp on the menu; (sirloin medallions and grilled shrimp, with sauteed asparagus, roasted garlic and mashed potatoes, topped with a lemon garlic pan jus).

It's quite obvious that the enthusiasm Jason shares with Bob about the Firehouse Grill cannot be extinguished.

DINERS INFORMATION

Address
4785 Lake Forest Dr., Cincinnati, OH 45242
www.firehousegrillcincinnati.com

Phone
(513) 733-3473

Hours
Monday - Thursday, 11:00 a.m. – 10:00 p.m.
Friday - Saturday, 11:00 a.m. – Midnight
Sunday, 11:00 a.m. – 9:00 p.m.

Price Range
$$

SOUTH WEST

179

The General Denver Hotel

N ot just a restaurant, but a pub in the middle of downtown Wilmington, The General Denver serves as the hub for business and social events in the community. Upon one of her frequent visits to this quaint mid-western town, Molly Dullea caught a glimpse of a this four-story building that had a faded For Sale sign in the window and had sat empty for way too long. After negotiating with the owner and on the basis of a handshake, Molly found herself as the new owner of this vintage 1928 hotel.

It is named in honor of General James William Denver, who was not only one of Wilmington's most venturesome citizens, but he also served as the governor of the "Bleeding Kansas Territory," was a Colorado legislator and the namesake of Denver, Colorado.

Molly and her husband, Mark, immediately began to revamp, remodel and redecorate the first floor restaurant, pub and entrance area. This Jacobeathan revival style structure was unlike any other in the area and now stands as a testament of will power, persistence and dedication to a long gone era. The Dulleas have also restored a number of single rooms and well appointed suites after they refurbished living quarters for their family.

This entrepreneur hired the best chef she could find, Jennifer Purky, and together they created an extensive seven page menu replete with mouth watering selections from appetizers, soups and salads, sandwiches and entrees. Tantalizing appetizers feature a selection of fries with a choice of toppings (bacon, ranch, cheese, chives), Greek Flatbread Pizza, the Denver Appetizer Combo (sweet po-

tato fries, onion straws and fried green beans with dipping sauce) as well as Quesadillas, and Spinach and Artichoke dip. Soups and salads include Black Bean Chili topped with cheese and red onions, and the delicious Harvest Chicken Salad is a tasty combination of fresh greens, apples, cranberries, and grilled chicken breast with Cranberry Apple Vinaigrette. All dressings, breads, and soups are homemade. Meat and produce are purchased from local farmers and from the year round Farmers Market located near the hotel. Specials are offered daily. Homemade desserts like gingerbread cake, Irish apple cake, German chocolate upside down cake, carrot cake and a variety of pies are a perfect end to a delicious meal.

The exquisitely designed bar serves every taste and not only carries popular brands of spirits and beer, but also a large selection of wines from local, state and international wineries. Frequent Draft Beer Weekends give visitors a chance to sample some of the local craft beers.

As a focal point of downtown activity, the hotel sponsors many popular events including: The Annual Wine Walk, frequent Block Parties, the October Ghost Walk, the Electric Parade, the Christmas Hometown Holidazzle, the Clinton County Open Hands Hog Roast Dinner, Earth Day Celebration, and tributes to literacy with the Reads Dinner and the Books n' More event.

This is a hopping place, and there is no telling *who* you might meet in the pub.

DINERS INFORMATION

Address
81 W. Main St., Wilmington, OH 45177
www.generaldenver.com

Phone
(937) 383-4141

Hours
Daily, 11:00 a.m. – closing varies

Price Range
$$

The Golden Lamb

Lebanon, OH

"With its legend of drama and romance that are a part of its traditions, The Golden Lamb is dedicated to the preservation of American life and holds fast to a quality of gentle and gracious living"

This succinct statement says it all about Ohio's oldest continuously operating hotel. In 1803, Jonas Seaman purchased a $4 license to operate a "house of public entertainment" and named it The Golden Lamb. In 1815, the building in which the restaurant and hotel currently occupies in downtown Lebanon was built and has been greatly expanded in order to accommodate the growing needs of the area and the business. It has been a popular stopping point for a host of prominent guests including 12 U.S. presidents including John Garfield, William McKinley, John Quincy Adams and, most recently, Ronald Reagan and George W. Bush.

I have eaten here many times throughout the years and enjoy the home cooking and warm atmosphere. As a history buff, I also enjoy learning more about life in Warren County 200 years ago. I always pick up a new tidbit of information before I leave.

Though the menu changes with the seasons, daily specials featured when I visited were the Roast Indiana Duckling with raspberry sauce served over wild rice, and the baked Red Snapper Creole. A house favorite is the Golden Lamb Skillet Fried Chicken and the Roast Butler County Turkey with onion sage dressing,

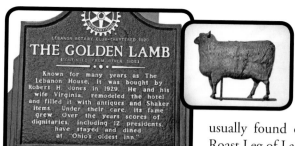

THE GOLDEN LAMB
(CONTINUED FROM OTHER SIDE)

Known for many years as The Lebanon House, it was bought by Robert H. Jones in 1929. He and his wife Virginia, remodeled the hotel and filled it with antiques and Shaker items. Under their care, its fame grew. Over the years scores of dignitaries, including 12 presidents, have stayed and dined at "Ohio's oldest inn."

which are quite popular and served with smashed potatoes and pan gravy. More traditional selections that are usually found on the menu are the Roast Leg of Lamb, which is quite fitting for a restaurant named The Golden Lamb, the Roasted Pork Loin and old-fashioned Smothered Swiss Steak.

The 8 oz. center cut Filet Mignon and slow roasted Prime Rib are regular features on the dinner menus. Not to be overshadowed by turf, delicacies from the surf include grilled Atlantic Salmon, and Shrimp and Scallop Fettuccine.

The Black Horse Tavern, where live music is regularly featured, is located toward the rear of the building with its own entrance. It is a great place to catch a bowl of soup and sandwich for lunch. I started out with an appetizer of Sauerkraut Balls served with spicy cocktail sauce and then had a delicious Chicken Salad Sandwich piled high with chunks of chicken, tomato and lettuce on thick home made white bread. A perfect finish was a piece of Sister Lizzy's Shaker Sugar Pie topped with caramel and a dollop of real whipped cream, and garnished with a sprig of mint. It is similar to Shoofly Pie without the pecans. And, yes, it was as scrumptious as it sounds!

You just cannot go wrong at The Golden Lamb no matter what you order; that's why it has been in business for over two centuries. There aren't too many places in North America that can make that claim. Oh, by the way, visit the unique gift shop on the lower level to pick up a keepsake before you leave.

DINERS INFORMATION

Address
27 S. Broadway St., Lebanon, OH 45036
www.goldenlamb.com

Phone
(513) 932-5065

Hours
Monday - Saturday, 11:00 a.m. – 9:00 p.m.
Sunday, Noon – 8:00 p.m.

Price Range
$$$

La Cascada

Hillsboro, OH

Conveniently located next to Kroger's parking lot in Hillsboro and across the street from Wal-Mart, this is a good place to catch a hardy meal before or after a shopping trip. The restaurant is upbeat and the hand-carved booths and chairs are decorated in brilliant rainbow colors that add an extra dose of sunshine. The scenes depicted are country themes, windmills, sunsets and farmers' fields with waves of golden grain. An exquisitely curved wood and stone bar was being installed when I visited, which has since added an exciting dimension to the place and provides extra seating. It was beautiful and I looked forward to another visit to see it already completed. There is plenty of parking in the large lot surrounding the restaurant, but go early because they do get busy.

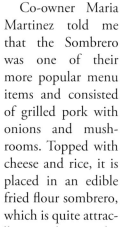

Co-owner Maria Martinez told me that the Sombrero was one of their more popular menu items and consisted of grilled pork with onions and mushrooms. Topped with cheese and rice, it is placed in an edible fried flour sombrero, which is quite attrac-

tive. The Arroz Con Pollo is another popular dish and is juicy grilled chicken breast with onions and mushrooms served on a bed of rice and topped with a creamy cheese sauce. As she tells it, the Crazy Burrito is a dish that customers go crazy over. It's a tortilla stuffed with rice, sour cream, chicken, steak strips, shrimp and onions and topped with cheese sauce and served with beans and guacamole sauce. The Rib Eye and T-bone steaks are a favorite as well as the seafood. I had the La Cascada Shrimp, which is a delicious medley of shrimp, crab meat, scallops, mushrooms, onions, spinach and tomatoes tossed in home made sauce and served over rice. It was an excellent blend of seafood and veggies.

The menu is quite extensive and should satisfy most any taste. I hope you visit some time soon.

DINERS INFORMATION

Address
140 Roberts Lane, Hillsboro, OH 45133
Phone
(937) 393-8861
Hours
Sunday - Thursday, 11:00 a.m. – 10:00 p.m.
Friday - Saturday, 11:00 a.m. – 11:00 p.m.
Sunday, 11:00 a.m. – 10:00 p.m.
Price Range
$

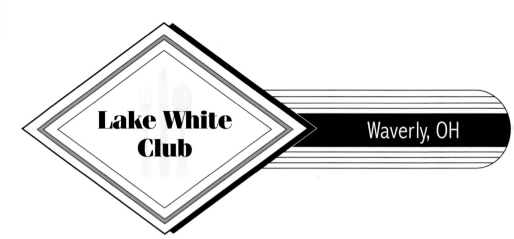

Lake White Club

Waverly, OH

In 1970, Dick and Audrey Ford purchased this fledging club on the shore of historic Lake White located in southern Ohio. It has long been a rural center of boating and swimming for area residents, as well as an Ohio governor or two. After Dick's death, Audrey sold the restaurant in 2011 to Jodi Harmon and David Crawford with the intention that the club's legacy, which dates back to the 1930s, would live on.

My husband and I have been regular diners at Lake White for years and have always found it to be a smooth spot in the otherwise bumpy road of life. I have not observed major changes since the transfer of ownership, except for a much-needed deck, but I'm sure that improvements are underway and will be ongoing. At this writing, the new owners have ambitious plans. Traditionally, the Club has been known for its family atmosphere and that has not changed. Children from one to a hundred are always welcome and are catered to by the staff.

The view from almost any window is awesome, especially on a summer evening when the air is clear and boaters are racing across the water often with a skier in tow or swimmers are paddling around close to shore. It's very relaxing.

The food is consistently good. I usually order the broiled fresh Deep Sea Scallops or the Fried Shrimp, which are very tasty. My husband enjoys the tender and juicy Filet or the New York Strip Steak cooked medium with a pink center. Each entrée includes a choice of tomato juice, soup, salad, potato and the vegetable of the day. A pile of thinly sliced breaded and deep fried onion rings also come with the meal and are always a hit. It seems like I can't get enough of them. The Fried Chicken became a trademark for the club back in 1936 and is still one of their most popular items. Now white or dark organic meat is available by choice.

The dessert that is most intriguing is the Post Mortem; both vanilla and coffee ice cream are served on a chocolate brownie and topped with chocolate sauce. It is indescribably delicious, but I wonder if the name reflects your state of being after you eat it. Hmmmm!

It will be exciting to see how this restaurant changes in the future, but it is a terrific place to get away from the cares of the world at any time.

SOUTH WEST

Los Mariachis

Chillicothe, OH

Located on the western side of town in a strip mall, this is one of the best Mexican restaurants of many located in Chillicothe. The atmosphere is festive, with authentic Mexican décor. The walls are decorated with sombreros and posters depicting bull fighting and other sights one might find while travelling through this country down south, and the colorful booths are eye popping with scenes of the Mexican countryside, village people, colorful birds and vivid rainbows.

Our son, Josh Paschke, helped build the restaurant when the previous owner converted it into a Mexican establishment. A few years later it became Los Mariachis. Our family has always enjoyed good meals and great service. The entrees are generous and hot, sometimes still sizzling when they come out of the kitchen and arrive at the table. The chip baskets and bottles of salsa are delivered as soon as we sit down and refilled frequently.

It's difficult to say what I favor, because I like almost everything on the menu. Enchiladas stuffed with beans and chicken covered with cheese sauce and salsa are delicious as is the deep fried Chimichanga stuffed with spicy beef and topped with cheese sauce, lettuce, sour cream, guacamole and pico de gallo. Unless

requested otherwise, beans and rice are usually included with most entrees. The prices are reasonable and there are combination plates for hardier appetites.

The language barrier sometimes becomes a problem, but the servers are patient and make sure they understand the order and any special requests that are made.

At this writing there are plans for another Los Mariachis to open up on the other side of town, which I suspect will be as good as this location.

Address
646 Central Center, Chillicothe, OH 45601
Phone
(740) 775-1403
Hours
Monday - Thursday, 11:00 a.m. – 10:00 p.m.
Friday - Saturday, 11:00 a.m. – 10:30 p.m.
Sunday, 11:00 a.m. – 9:30 p.m.
Price Range
$

Moyer Winery and Restaurant

Manchester, OH

"Come, Relax and Enjoy." This sign beckons those passing by this out of the way restaurant and winery bordered by five acres of vineyards, the Ohio River, and U.S. #52 east of Cincinnati near the village of Manchester. After a pleasant afternoon enjoying exquisite culinary creations and the breathtaking view of the river, I fully agree with the greeting. A gazebo provides a picturesque location to capture the moment with the river rolling in the background. The wooden balcony on the second floor has removable walls, that not only enhances the view but also allows guests to enjoy summer breezes. This is definitely white tablecloth, fine dining that is provided in both the spacious dining room and on the deck, which are both wheelchair accessible.

Co-owner Tom Hamrick told me the story of how Ken Moyer decided to turn his full-time attention from engineering to wine making back in 1973 when he and his wife Mary bought the former truck stop and featured only French bread, bean, bacon and cheese soup along with wine tasting from their locally produced reserves. Ken had created the bean soup in his dorm room, but he had a long way to go to become an expert vintner. Over the next 26 years, they not only expanded their menu, but as they became more experienced winemakers, they added to their wine list as well. In 1999, they sold the restaurant and winery to a group of friends who have maintained the fine Moyer's reputation.

Far from the original fare of bean soup and cheese, the menu now features breaded and deep-fried chicken livers served over wild rice, River Val-

ley Salmon nested on creamy whipped potatoes and topped with asparagus and hollandaise sauce, and the Blue Jacket pan-blackened chicken served with summer squash and blue cheese cream sauce. The Derby Brown is Moyer's version of the Kentucky favorite, which is an open-faced turkey sandwich on grilled sour dough bread topped with cheddar and parmesan mornay sauce, bacon and tomato.

There is also a selection of fresh hand cut steaks, from an 8 oz. filet mignon and a choice of two rib eye dishes to the Vineyard Filet Portobello and seared Beef Medallions as well as Surf & Turf (6 oz. mignon with Cajun fired Gulf shrimp).

To balance off the menu, shrimp and salmon is prepared in a Chardonnay cream sauce, Bechamel Poached Scallops casserole is wrapped in whipped potatoes with a wine sauce and Swiss cheese, and for the undecided the Rivers by Seafood provides a combination of shrimp, scallops, crab cake and baked cheddar cheese grits.

A selection of more than a dozen award-winning wines that are produced on site near the restaurant can be sampled at the table and can be ordered by the glass or the bottle.

Like its 30,000 bottles of wine produced each year, Moyer Winery has matured into an elegant dining experience for the hungry and thirsty traveler.

DINERS INFORMATION

Address
3859 U.S. 52, Manchester, OH 45144
www.moyerwinery.com

Phone
(937) 549-2957

Hours
Monday - Thursday, 11:30 a.m. – 9:00 p.m.
Friday - Saturday, 11:30 a.m. – 10:00 p.m.
Sunday, 11:30 a.m. – 5:00 p.m. (May - October)
Monday - Friday, 4:00 p.m. – 6:00 p.m. (Early Bird Special - 2 dinners for $20)

Price Range
$$$

Murphin Ridge Inn

West Union, OH

If you are looking for a laid back atmosphere on the top of one of Adam County's tallest hills, Murphin Ridge is the place. The resort is surrounded by 140 acres of wooded trails, open fields and scenic natural landscapes that can inspire, relax or reenergize. Visitors can enjoy an evening meal or stay for the week. Both options are priced accordingly, but the main appeal here is the feeling that the cares of life are far away. Nestled in the comfort of the countryside, one can see deer grazing, turkeys gobbling and pheasants flying in the area. The patio overlooks the herb and vegetable gardens, where a variety of produce is grown to be used in the tasty dishes featured in the primitive 1820s Farm House that serves as the restaurant. I was enamored with the antique wishing well where many visitors had cast their future dreams to the wind and wishfully tossed coins into the depths. I wondered how many had come true.

Vintage buildings abound on the property along with a log cabin, but owners Sherry and Darryl McKenney have built nine rustic woodland cabins with modern bathrooms and fireplaces for the comfort and privacy of their guests.

"Retreat, recharge, refuel and refresh" is the slogan at Murphin Ridge and the McKenneys have provided for each, especially from the kitchen. The limited menu provides seasonal items including stuffed cannelloni (Will's Harvest), a 12 oz rib eye steak (Red Dog's Favorite), pork chops and chicken. Each entrée is served with soup, salad and items that come from the Murphin Ridge garden. Smaller portions are available and feature selections are Prime Steak BBQ, pizza, homemade soup of the day and salad. A full bar allows for alcoholic or non-alcoholic drinks to complement the meal. Meat, chicken and fish are purchased locally as are organic eggs from the nearby Amish market.

It is rare to have the chance to just relax in such natural beauty, but this is the place to let your hair down.

DINERS INFORMATION

Address
750 Murphin Ridge Road, West Union, OH 45693
www.murphinridgeinn.com

Phone
(877) 687-7446 / (937) 544-2263

Hours
Tuesday - Saturday, 5:30 p.m. – 8:00 p.m. (dinner)

Price Range
$$$

SOUTH WEST

Old Canal Smoke House

Chillicothe, OH

The Old Canal Smoke House is very near where the historic Ohio and Erie Canal once carried freight traffic the full length of the state from Cleveland to Portsmouth in the 1800s, and owners Dane and Jodie Straub have transformed this old house on the corner to a spectacular and elegant restaurant complete with a covered patio that seats guests three seasons out of the year.

Not only is the Smoke House well known in Ross County for its hickory smoked barbeque ribs, pulled pork and brisket, but people all over the region and beyond travel to Chillicothe to get a taste of that sweet sauce. This is an active hub for shopping, the Paints Frontier League baseball games, and boating on the Scioto River, so the restaurant fits right in to feed hungry active people, and those not so active too! Barbeque always reminds me of family picnics as a kid when we barbequed everything and messed our faces digging into that juicy sauce covered meat. So dig in and enjoy.

Ribeye Steak, Prime Rib, and Atlantic Salmon are all smoked to perfection and served with a choice of sides, like Green Bean Almondine, Corn Casserole, Smoke House Ranch Fries and Spuds (real hand mashed potatoes with sour cream and fried onions). Only certified Angus beef is served to

assure the highest quality meat.

And how could anyone pass up scrumptious desserts like a Grilled Pineapple with Ice Cream that is dipped in coconut milk, grilled and then sprinkled with cinnamon and sugar. The Strawberry Tart in a fluffy pastry with a cheesecake center is simply fantastic and offsets the heaviness of the meal. Even the Cheesecake (New York style or lemon) is light and fluffy, but filled with flavor.

A visit to the Old Canal Smoke House is certainly worth the trip.

DINERS INFORMATION

Address
94 E. Water St., Chillicothe, OH 45601
Phone
(740) 779-3278
Hours
Monday - Saturday   11:00 a.m. – 11:00 p.m.
Closed Sunday
Covered patio seating weather permitting
Price Range
$$

The Old Y Restaurant

Chickens, chickens everywhere...on the wallpaper, on the shelves, in baskets and even in stained glass windows. But according to Susan, the manager, more chickens grace the place than one would find in nearby hen houses. When Jamie and Susan Hauke bought the establishment, they cleared out some of the theme decorations to provide a fresh look, which long time customers said they appreciated. According to Susan, "Our regulars thought that it was overdone and we did too. Now they come in to enjoy our buffet and order from the menu."

The Old Y has a legacy dating back to the 1950s, when the main attraction was a commercial plane that was attached to the main dining facility. Tables were set up and guests could eat in the airplane, which was quite a novelty for the area. Eventually the plane was hauled away and the chick-

196

ens remained along with a white gazebo that marks the entrance of the restaurant on Route 62.

Visitors drive in from Cincinnati, Columbus, Jeffersonville and other areas far and wide in order to eat the broasted chicken and enjoy homemade pies that melt in your mouth. The draw used to be the plane, but now it is just plain and simple good food

Though there are daily specials like meatloaf, beef and noodles, homemade chicken and noodles, and baked steak, the buffet features "made from scratch" rice pudding and cole slaw along with a variety of other salads, meats and desserts. Pies are baked daily and include custard, coconut cream, peanut butter, butterscotch, Boston cream along with a host of fresh fruit pies as well. The beef used for steaks, burgers, and roast beef is locally raised and butchered with careful attention to the type of feed used that results in marbling which improves the quality of the meat.

This is a nice, no frills diner conveniently located on St. Rt. 62 between Hillsboro and Sardinia, but they provide good wholesome food to their customers.

Address
1940 US Rt. 62 South, Winchester, Ohio 45697

Phone
(937) 442-3222

Hours
Daily, 6:00 a.m. – 9:00 p.m.

Price Range
$

The Portsmouth Brewing Company

Portsmouth, OH

"May your glass be ever full, may the roof over your head be always strong, and may you be in heaven half an hour before the devil knows you're dead." (Old Irish Toast)

Just a few yards from the Ohio River and beside the beautiful Portsmouth murals stands the Portsmouth Brewing Company, which I have included in this book because of the historical significance to Ohio and the quality of the food that the restaurant serves. I am not a beer drinker, but I found the tour through the brewery fascinating because it dates back to the 1800s. After being closed for a number of years in the early 1900s during and after Prohibition, it was eventually reestablished as a functional brewery. I will feature the details of this location in the upcoming book on *Places to Visit in Ohio,* but for now let it suffice that it is an interesting place to spend

an afternoon before taking in a fine meal at the restaurant.

As a book dedicated to excellence in eating, I was concerned whether the menu could compete with the great food I have found in so many Ohio eateries. I was pleasantly surprised that it could. So with this entry I am combining casual dining in an historic setting that may also be fascinating to you, the reader.

The Brewing Company offers a wide selection of good food that is not the typical bar food. Their specialty is Prime Rib prepared daily by coating a whole piece with a special blend of seasonings and cooking it slowly in order to keep it moist and juicy. Then it is cut and prepared to order in two sizes: the 12 oz. Queen Cut and the 16 oz. King Cut. Their Spaghetti with Cheese tossed in their homemade sauce is prepared a little differently than I make it at home. After covering it in mozzarella cheese, it is baked until golden brown before serving. The intermingling of the sauce, melted cheese and the noodles makes for a slightly tangy, but delicious dish.

Their Lasagna is unique as well in that they alternate layers of al dente lasagna noodles with their homemade meat sauce, creamy mixture of cheeses and house spices to create a blend of flavors that is sure to please. Beer Battered Chicken Wings is another favorite that customers love. They are lightly coated with a beer batter and then deep fried and served with celery sticks and choice of dressing or BBQ sauce.

Pizza, sandwiches and salads are also available as is the children's menu, which features the spaghetti, lasagna and chicken strips. This is a family place where everyone, young and younger, will enjoy.

DINERS INFORMATION

Address
224 Second Street, Portsmouth, OH 45662
Phone
(740) 354-6106
Hours
Monday - Thursday, 11:00 a.m. – 10:00 p.m.
Friday - Saturday, 11:00 a.m. – 11:00 p.m.
Sunday, Noon – 10:00 p.m.
Price Range
$

SOUTH WEST

Located in downtown Portsmouth a few blocks from the Ohio River, The Ribber is a well known hangout not just for the town's residents, but for many who have heard of its reputation for ribs, steaks and chicken. In fact, I had a number of referrals to this restaurant from people all over the state, so I had to see for myself whether it was everything it was cracked up to be. I met with owners Darren and Jennifer Mault who were very pleasant, helpful and informative. Darren's parents, Steve and Cornelia, opened The Ribber in 1978 after Steve retired from the Air Force where he learned, among other things, to smoke food. The hours of the restaurant were limited at first, but have expanded to seven days a week. Being family owned, you can be sure that one of the family members is in the restaurant all the time.

The size of the place is deceptive from the outside, but you enter through the bar and the dining room is in back. There is a more secluded dining area all the way in the back of the building where overflow customers can be seated away from the crush of the crowds and the sound of the bar area.

The house specialties are the ribs (thus the name – The Ribber) and steaks as well as chicken, which I sampled. The ribs were large, meaty and fell of the bone, and could be eaten easily with a fork or, if you are a real rib eating aficionado, picked up and eaten like corn on the cob. The size of the order varies from a petite (one piece rib dinner) to large (four piece dinner) depending on how hungry you are. The

New York Strip steak (ribeyes are also available) was cooked to perfection at medium well and was tender, juicy and full of flavor. It was an excellent piece of meat and the chef knew how to sear the outside to capture the juices on the insides. Excellent! There are two sizes to choose from; the small steak is a reasonable 16 ounces and the large steak is a whopping 32 ounces.

I also sampled the chicken breast, which was moist and not overcooked. This sometimes happens with white meat, but the dark meat was juicy and savory, too. The side order of barbeque sauce gave an excellent sweet and spicy flavor that highlighted the taste of the meat.

All dinners are served with a choice of potato (baked or fries), onion rings as well as German slaw or creamy cole slaw, green beans or baked beans. The hand cut Ribber fries are excellent as is the homemade German cole slaw. Fresh daily peanut butter or cream pies are a perfect compliment to the end of the meal. If you can't eat it there, they'll box up a piece to take home.

Based on my experience, The Ribber is everything it was cracked up to be – the food, the service, the atmosphere. It has certainly lived up to its reputation in my book.

DINERS INFORMATION

Address
1024 Gallia Street, Portsmouth, OH 45662
www.theribber.com

Phone
(740) 353-9329

Hours
Monday, 11:00 a.m. – 9:00 p.m.
Tuesday - Saturday, 11:00 a.m. – 10:00 p.m.
Sunday, Noon – 9:00 p.m.

Price Range
$

Spillway Lodge

Clarksville, OH

In 1973, Clarence and Jane Benney moved from Loveland, Ohio, to the countryside of Wilmington. It was there where they found a lovely house at auction surrounded by acres of rolling hills and rich Ohio farmland that was situated on the edge of a spillway from Cowan Lake. It was a perfect place for Clarence and Jane to raise their five children, have ponies and entertain their friends. The house also accommodated Jane's extensive antique doll collection as well as her extensive collection of Depression glass, which is still on display today in the restaurant. The Benneys soon decided that it would be an ideal location for a restaurant. They redecorated and added on a 20 x 40 foot deck that accommodates large parties spilling out from the party room. Today more than 125 people can be seated in the main dining room and the party room.

In 1986, their son, Steve, became the owner and main chef. He has continued the legacy of his parents and has maintained the reputation of this excellent out of the way steakhouse known for its fine food and excellent service. Steve buys produce and meat locally, cuts his own steaks and cooks them to order. Filet mignon, New York Strip, and chopped sirloin topped with sautéed mushrooms or red peppers and onions are most popular. The prime rib is tender and baked to perfection or charbroiled to enhance the flavor.

Not to be ignored is the extensive selec-

tion of seafood. Shrimp the size of a baseball is prepared in a variety of dishes and includes grilled shrimp on skewers with drawn butter, fried shrimp, and the Shrimp Trio (scampi, grilled and stuffed). The Alaskan King crab legs literally melt in your mouth and the tender salmon is glazed with a honey Teriyaki sauce. While there is not an extensive selection, their delectable homemade strawberry pie tops the list.

The décor is rustic and is reminiscent of Steve's parents' taste from the period in which they were owners. Thick-beamed ceilings and posts with hard wood floors reminded me of vacations lodges I visited as a child.

As I sat at the table, the water rushed through the spillway as an early spring snow fell and clung to the trees and the grass. This lovely sight added an elegant sparkle to the surroundings that topped off a delightful evening. The Spillway Lodge is a unique combination of great food provided in the comfort of a traditional setting.

DINERS INFORMATION

Address
623 Old State Road, Clarksville, OH 45113

Phone
(937) 289-2168

Hours
Tuesday - Thursday, 5:00 p.m. – 10:00 p.m.
Saturday - Saturday, 11:30 a.m. – 9:00 p.m.
Closed Monday
Specialties: Steak & Seafood

Price Range
$$$

SOUTH EAST
REGION

The Galley	Marietta, OH
Grouse Nest Restaurant	South Bloomingville, OH
Gunroom Restaurant	Marietta, OH
Levee House Café	Marietta, OH
Millstone BBQ	Logan, OH
Oak Room	Athens, OH
The Olde Dutch Restaurant	Logan, OH
Restaurant Salaam	Athens, OH
The Ridge Inn	Laurelville, OH
The Sandstone	Logan, OH
Zoe	Athens, OH

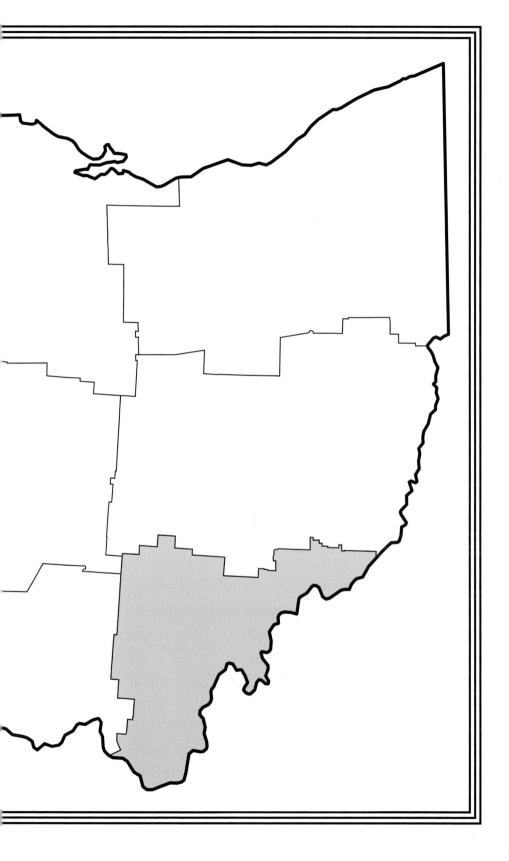

The Galley

Marietta, OH

The turn of the century in Marietta was booming, thanks to a surge in oil and gas production, and the Hatchett Hotel, the current home of The Galley was built in 1899. The entire city was transformed from a sleepy little burg to a thriving town almost over night. Local oil entrepreneur John Hatchett converted the first floor of his hotel to a saloon and a bowling alley, where he sold five cent beer and ten cent whiskey.

After a number of renovations to the building, The Adventure Galley was established in 1981. Twenty-five years later, extensive additions were made and The Galley was born. Once again with an eye to the future, another transformation took place on the other side of the building in 2010 that created a center of entertainment downtown called The Adelphia, where live music is featured and popular movies are shown regularly. During special events dinner and drinks are available, too.

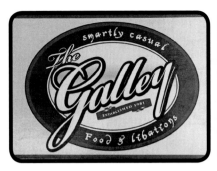

The Galley has an Irish Pub atmosphere, but offers American regional specialties and the highest quality steaks and seafood. Original recipes are created by the chef with a unique blend of flavors that satisfies even the most discerning taste. There are sandwiches and wraps as well as burgers and pasta, but the big draw here is the grass fed, premium Black Angus steaks. From the Flat Iron Steak, the 12 oz. choice cut Ribeye to the tender 8 oz. hand cut Filet Mignon (or the 6 oz. Petit), guests come from miles around to experience the succulent taste of any one of these fine pieces of beef.

Not to be ignored, the seafood is stiff competition featuring the Wasabi Encrusted Tuna served over scallions and baby shrimp fried rice, stir fried veggies and finished with pickled onions. Then there is the fresh cut, seared Atlantic Salmon basted with honey butter and lemon and served over rice pilaf. Can it get any better than this? Well, perhaps. The Black Tiger Shrimp is roasted in Hoisin sauce (a Chinese dipping sauce) and served on Asian slaw.

Remember to top your delicious meal off with one of the pastry chef's house-made desserts. Take your pick of a number of cakes — the Perfect Chocolate Cake, Snickers Cheesecake, or Carrot Cake — or the Seasonal Cobbler. But my favorite is the Pumpkin Crème Brulee. No matter what you choose, you can't lose.

This is an exciting place and has so much to offer in many categories.

DINERS INFORMATION

Address
203 Second St., Marietta, OH 45750
www.thegalleymarietta.com

Phone
(740) 374-8278

Hours
Monday - Thursday, 11:00 a.m. – 9:00 p.m.
Friday - Saturday, 11:00 a.m. – 10:00 p.m.
Closed Sunday

Price Range
$$

SOUTH EAST

Grouse Nest Restaurant

South Bloomingville, OH

The Hocking Hills area was formed during the icebergs that pushed their way through southern Ohio. The Grouse Nest Restaurant is located in a beautiful wooded setting at the Hocking Hills Resort on top of a ridge and at the end of a steep gravel drive, where I was thankful to have my 4-wheel drive vehicle. When I arrived I discovered that this was more than a restaurant; it is a resort where one can visit for the afternoon or evening or stay for a week and enjoy hiking, relaxing or soaking in the hot tub. Through rain or snow, lunch and dinner is served year round in the bright and refreshing dining room with white tablecloths and vases of fresh flowers on every table. In warmer weather, outside dining is delightful where the tables are surrounded by flower gardens and a gazebo with a great view of the valley and nearby hills.

Meals are home made using locally grown produce along with wild game native to Ohio, like venison, quail, rabbit, rattlesnake and boar, which was introduced by Chef Miller. American cuisine is served, as they say, with a gourmet twist. Some of the unique entrees include Jambalaya Snake, Apricot Quail, Lobster Ravioli, spicy Elk Sopressata (a southern Italian culinary favorite), Veni-

zon Hamburger and Medallions, Buffalo Chicken and boneless Chicken Wings. In addition to soup du jour there are also delectable desserts du jour like Crème Brule, Chocolate Mousse and Smore's Cupcake. Specials for under $10 are offered nightly. And a full bar with top shelf spirits helps quench the thirst during the daily Happy Hour which often features live music.

Dress is casual in this family friendly place where children are welcome and get their own menu. But after a long day of travelling if you're too tired to come to the restaurant, your meal can come to you at the nearby cottages. The restaurant will cater meals for both small and large groups who can enjoy a good meal and relax in the laid back environment. The Jack in the Pulpit Room accommodates groups up to 40 guests and the reception hall seats up to 225 guests.

Grouse Nest was one of the first restaurants in the area that provided fine dining in a casual setting. The brainchild of Randy and Melody Strickland who opened the restaurant in 2001, they have expanded by including a number of buildings – even the Hocking Hills Chapel.

So whether you are travelling as a couple or more, this is a place not to miss.

DINERS INFORMATION

Address
25780 Liberty Hill Road, South Bloomingville, OH 43152
www.grousenest.com

Phone
(740) 332-4501

Hours
Thursday - Sunday, 11:30 a.m. – 9:00 p.m.

Price Range
$$

Gunroom Restaurant

The Gunroom Restaurant, located in the historic Lafayette Hotel on the edge of the Ohio River, is a Marietta tradition and unique dining experience. Manager Sheila Rhodes has seen many changes since she started with the restaurant in 1996, and she especially enjoys meeting the many guests that travel from all parts of the country, even internationally.

A major event in town is the Ohio River Sternwheel Festival that takes place the weekend after Labor Day each year. Sheila said that thousands of people are in town to watch or participate and the hotel is booked two years in advance. Activity in the Gun Room picks up as well.

Established in 1918 at the same time the hotel was built, the Gun Room is decorated in 19th century riverboat décor and derives its name from an extensive long rifle collection displayed in the dining room. The restaurant is a versatile part of the hotel and features live music and special events like the Murder Mystery Weekend and wine tasting parties.

The menu is most impressive, with a delicious variety of selections in each category. Rolls, soups and desserts are made fresh daily. And the seafood entrees include seared Scallops Florentine, Beer Battered Shrimp and broiled Red Snapper. We sampled the Crab Cakes that were made with chunks of lump crab, broiled to a golden brown and finished with a lemon aioli, which is a garlic mayonnaise. The crab, which was sweet and rich with flavor, was served with garlic, red skin

The Gun Room

mashed potatoes that were an excellent complement.

The hand cut and "flame kissed" Angus steaks include the 12 oz. New York Strip, the 16 oz. Porterhouse and the Ribeye, as well as the 10 oz. Louisiana Sirloin and the 6 oz. Flat Iron, which is the shoulder cut of the beef. All can be enhanced with a choice of Cabernet sauces, melted crumbled bleu cheese, sautéed mushrooms and onions or blackened for extra flavor.

A few of the classic entrees include tender Baby Beef Liver, a Sweet-n-Sour French Cut Pork Chop and the Chipotle Pasta. We tried the Fetuccini Alfredo with Parmesan cheese, and it was excellent. The Alfredo sauce was light and creamy and the Fetuccini was tender but not soggy. Most entrees are served with a choice of potato and vegetable, but the a la carte menu offers additional choices like steak fries, rice pilaf, cole slaw, onion rings and apple sauce to name only a few.

A reasonably priced children's menu offers Chicken Fingers, Spaghetti and Marinara, Pita Pizza, Popcorn Shrimp and a children's portion of Sirloin Steak. Dessert, like Cheesecake, Brad Pudding, Crème Brulee and the Flourless Chocolate Torte can be ordered from the main menu.

Dining in the Gun Room is like stepping back in time as is staying in one of the beautiful rooms of the Lafayette Hotel where each room is decorated in classic antiques. It is a unique experience and certainly not one to be missed whether you visit for the Sternwheel Festival or one of the other events taking place by the river.

DINERS INFORMATION

Address
101 Front Street, Marietta, OH 45750
www.lafayettehotel.com

Phone
(740) 373-5522

Hours
Daily, 9:00 a.m. – 5:00 p.m.

Price Range
$$$

Levee House Café

Marietta, OH

This is *Ohio Magazine's* Top Ten Favorite Restaurants and for good reason. The food is excellent, the staff is attentive, and the location is perfect. Situated along the walking path upriver from the historic Lafayette Hotel, the view of the river is outstanding and very relaxing as we sat on the patio with a cup of coffee watching the world go by. What a great little place!

The dining room has limited space, which provides a more intimate atmosphere, but it might be wise to call ahead to see how busy they are. Owners Kim and David Hearing are pleasant and dedicated. He is the head chef and creates most of the dishes served at the Levee House. Full-time mom Kim, who had worked for a major restaurant chain, lends her advice and assistance when needed.

They have created a full service restaurant with a focus on healthy dishes and fresh ingredients featuring deliciously different home made soups, salads, pizzas, pastas and dinner entrees.

One of the most popular dishes David is particularly proud of is the Crab and Shrimp Cake, with lump crab and baby shrimp topped with roasted pepper and horseradish sauce. Horseradish is also a main ingredient in the Crusted Salmon. Cheese and special house sauces play an important part in the tender Crusted Beef Medallions made with melted bleu cheese, and the Chicken Piccata served in a white wine sauce. The Nut Crusted Chicken is stuffed with goat cheese and rolled in crunchy nutty breading and topped with a sundried tomato cream. And there is the Blackened Chicken Pasta, which, according to David, creates a perfect balance in taste. The Root Beer Tenderloin is actually marinated in root beer, which gives it a subtle sweet taste, but is offset by the onion it is cooked in.

Desserts are also home made and delectable. The flourless chocolate cake with dairy free whipped cream drizzled in raspberry sauce is perfect for those allergic to wheat/gluten and dairy. They don't have to forgo their sweet tooth. On the other hand, the Cloudless Chocolate Cake, Crème Brulee and the Bananas Foster satisfy the craving for sweets for the rest of the guests.

A limited selection of wine and beer are on hand to compliment most any dish, as are ice tea and soft drinks. Convenient parking is available across the street or behind the building.

When you are visiting Marietta, this is a must place to have lunch or dinner.

DINERS INFORMATION

Address
127 Ohio Street, Marietta, OH 45750
Check them out on Facebook

Phone
(740) 374-2233

Hours
Daily, 11:00 a.m. – 2:00 p.m. (lunch);
5:00 p.m. – 9:00 p.m. (dinner)

Price Range
$$

Millstone BBQ

Logan, OH

Millstone is the center of fun in this small community. Regularly scheduled events take place almost every night and bring people together – old friends and total strangers – especially in the summer. From May through October, weather permitting, every Tuesday is Bike Night when there is live music on the patio, giveaways and, according to the hype, "the friendliest gathering of bikers and non-bikers anywhere." Other events held on site are car shows, the Little Miss contest, the Summer Fest Queen contest, the Smokin' Hot Summer Fest and the Warrior Dash.

This rustic building was constructed in 2006 using raw, naturally aged beams from area barns. It has an open floor plan that still provides privacy, though one can see the flat screen HD TVs from almost any seat in the house. And there is a sense of being on the farm from the initial greeting of the large steer's head on the wall by the entrance and the ceramic pig sitting by the door to the display of old plows, barrels and wheels around the restaurant safely situated above the heads of the guests. This is also the largest restaurant in Hocking County with a full service bar.

I noticed a party atmosphere as soon as I walked in, though all I heard was recorded classic rock. The enthusiasm of the co-managers, Mandy Reeves and Adam Wetzel, was contagious. While we talked, they bounced ideas off of each other as to how they could create new events, more contests and activities, as well as unique dishes and drinks. Both have been with Millstone almost from the beginning and appear to be a compatible team. Bottom line is that they love their job and they try to make every guest feel welcome.

Millstone is known for its southern smoked BBQ, and all meats are smoked on site for 15 to 17 hours with a dry rub, which is a mix of seasonings that are rubbed on the outside of the meat before it is smoked over shag bark hickory. I was told that the key indicator to look for is the pink hue inside the meat, which is called the smoke ring. This means that the meat is moist and tender, and ready to serve. I found this to be true when I tried the BBQ ribs that were so tender they fell off the bone and the pulled pork that melted in my mouth. Turkey and chicken are not left out of the smoking process and appear on the menu in floured tortilla wraps, club sandwiches, and on the bone (half a chicken) or sliced. The homemade bread pudding is delicious.

They offer take-out, delivery and occasionally cater events. According to Mandy and Adam, Millstone is where "southern hospitality is brought north." and their goal is to "greet everyone warmly so that they go home with a satisfied smile. We hope that our service, fun atmosphere and unique flavors will call you to visit again and again."

DINERS INFORMATION

Address
12790 Grey St., Logan, Ohio 43138
www.millstonebbq.com

Phone
(740) 385-5341

Hours
Monday - Thursday, 11:00 a.m. — 9:00 p.m.
Friday - Saturday, 11:00 a.m. — 10:30 p.m.
Sunday, 10:00 a.m. — 9:00 p.m.
Sunday Bruch, 10:00 a.m. — 1:00 p.m.

Price Range
$$

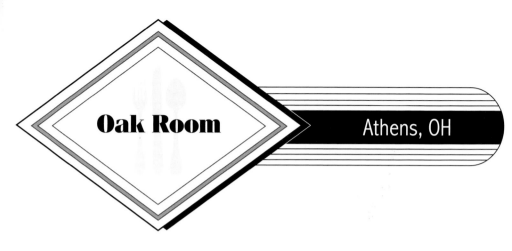

Oak Room

Athens, OH

This cozy family owned and managed restaurant and tavern is located only minutes from the Ohio University campus and offers a variety of dishes to help refuel the tank for an upcoming exam, catch a sandwich with friends or just celebrate the end of the term. There are daily specials and a lunch buffet during the week, with Prime Rib served on Friday and Saturday nights. From soup and burgers to New York Strip Steak and Turkey Reubens, even a student on a tight budget can afford a meal here.

The French Onion soup is thick and cheesy and the Chicken Breast Salad is fresh and crispy, with a sizeable piece of tender chicken covered with Ranch dressing. The Ion's Burger is a tender 5 oz. Angus burger topped with mushrooms, onions and provolone cheese and served on a pretzel bun. The Four Cheese Penne is the Oak Room's version of baked creamy mac and cheese garnished with chives and diced tomatoes. It was delicious, with a slightly

sharp taste from the combination of cheeses. And one of the unique dishes I had was the Baked Brie smothered in honey and served with crostini. It was a great blend between the sweetness of the honey and the crunchiness of the bread. The Oak Room Potato Chips were excellent and were not what I expected. Instead they were thick slices of deep-fried potatoes with melted cheddar cheese and ranch sauce. Very tasty indeed.

The Oak Room is spacious with a split-level floor plan that has a second floor balcony to accommodate overflow guests on nights when there is live music. The main floor is divided into a two dining areas, with tables and booths. The bar room is centrally located and decorated with an extensive collection of colorful beer keg taps. A wide variety of beers and micro brews are served daily and Happy Hour is from 3:00 to 7:00.

DINERS INFORMATION

Address
14 Station St., Athens, OH 45701
www.oakroom.net

Phone
(740) 593-8386

Hours
Monday - Friday, 11:00 a.m. – 9:30 p.m.
Saturday, Noon – 9:30 p.m.
Closed Sunday
Bar has extended hours

Price Range
$$

The Olde Dutch Restaurant

Logan, OH

As the realtors say, what sells is "location, location, location," and this restaurant has that market cornered. Located right off State Route 33 in southeastern Ohio between Lancaster and Athens in the historic Rempel's Grove complex, it is a concentrated area for shopping and other activities. A visitor can check out the Logan Craft and Antique Malls, buy Amish products at the Country Cupboard Bulk Food store, take a cruise from the Hocking Hills Canoe Livery, commune with albino deer and miniature goats at the petting zoo or test one's skill at the Adventure Miniature Golf Course. And a lovely gift shop with wooden gifts along with other souvenirs is located in the restaurant lobby. The entire area is very unique and is sure to please the entire family.

The restaurant offers an Amish style meal complete with fresh baked rolls and bread and a selection of desserts. It was a difficult decision to choose from the many items featured on the daily buffet, which included the browned and broasted chicken (the house specialty), tender roast beef, tangy barbequed pork, creamy chicken and noodles, and homemade ham loaf and a wide choice of side dishes. But I did go for the mashed potatoes and gravy and the sweet stewed tomatoes, which were delicious. Even the fried chicken livers were tender and tasty. Additional choices can be found on the full menu.

With a seating capacity of almost 300, groups are welcome and there is ample bus/RV parking. The Oak Room, named for the exquisite oak trim that abounds in the downstairs banquet room highlighted with beautiful stained glass doors, accommodates another 180 visitors. In order to handle the ever-growing traffic, the downstairs was excavated and completed in 2002.

I met Mike Erb, who joined the staff in 1997 three years after the restaurant opened, and after a successful career in corporate America, he eventually became general manager of the Olde Dutch. He devotes long hours attending to every detail from the kitchen to the dining room, which is quite evident not only in the quality and consistency of the food but in the contentment of the staff, most of whom are long term employees.

The Olde Dutch is definitely a worthwhile stop when you are on your way to a rocking good time in Hocking Hills.

DINERS INFORMATION

Address
12791 St. Rt. 664, Logan, OH 43138
www.oldedutch.com

Phone
(740) 385-1000

Hours

Winter (Nov. - April)	Monday - Saturday, 11:00 a.m. – 8:00 p.m.
	Sunday, 11:00 a.m. – 7:00 p.m.
Summer (May - Oct.)	Monday - Thursay, 11:00 a.m. – 8:00 p.m.
	Friday, 11:00 a.m. – 9:00 p.m.
	Saturday, 8:00 a.m. – 9:00 p.m.
	Sunday, 8:00 a.m. – 8:00 p.m.

Price Range
$

Restaurant Salaam

Athens, OH

This restaurant offers fine cuisine inspired by the food of the Middle East, North Africa and the Indian subcontinent with an extensive selection of beers and wine from all over the world served in an exotic yet family-friendly atmosphere. What a wonderful dining experience, surrounded by an eclectic collection of Pakistani Ralli quilts on the wall, Suzani textiles, and Moroccan lamps, all mementos that owners Hilarie and Mark Burhns have collected in their travels.

This is a delightful place located in downtown Athens not far from the Ohio University main campus. Voted the Best of Athens, and the Best Ethnic Cuisine as well as second best Vegetarian Cuisine and Fine Dining restaurant, Salaam combines atmosphere with excellent food and refreshing beverages, especially their mint green tea.

Their lunch and dinner menus feature numerous daily specials, including vegetarian and vegan entrees, but lamb, chicken and beef entrees are also featured. I started out with fried Falafel patties, which are seasoned and ground chick peas with tahini-lemon sauce, as well as a hot creamy artichoke parmesan spread with warm homemade bread for dipping. I also ate one of my favorites: Dolmas, which are rice stuffed grape leaves with fresh lemon and olive oil. As a salad, I chose Tabouli, which is a bulghur wheat salad with veggies, and a tasty combination of lemon, parsley and mint. It was a bit spicy but had a rich flavor. As my entrée the toasted Coconut Curry Chicken sounded good especially served with basmati rice, coriander chutney and cu-

cumber raita, which was delicious. Hilarie told me that she uses cardamom and cinnamon in many recipes to achieve a subtle sweet taste rather than using cane sugar. She also stores her spices whole, which assures a longer shelf life, until she toasts and freshly grinds them in an Indian grinder as she prepares her dishes. Dessert was a delicate, crispy piece of Baklava, a walnut, cinnamon and cardamom confectionary. All but the flat bread is made fresh daily. And locally grown pastry flour is ground by a fifth generation family mill located in nearby Logan.

Hilarie and Mark joined me for lunch which gave me the benefit of learning more about the ingredients in her dishes and the way she prepares them. I marveled at her knowledge about spices and the part they play in her cooking. Mark, who plays a mean fiddle, and Hilarie, who plays the banjo, often provide music for their guests, but usually she is the creative food artist in the kitchen who is refining a recipe, often one that was suggested by a guest or one of her own originals.

When Hilarie and Mark met in high school and eventually married they had no idea how exciting their life would be as they proceeded on a journey that took them to all parts of the world. They eventually settled in Athens in 2009. After managing a small hookah establishment, the Shishah Café, they changed their focus to a more culinary focused venture with Salaam.

The Ridge Inn

Laurelville, OH

"The Best Food in Laurelville!"

The Ridge Inn began with an inspiration that Jo Eaves had to start a business in this small town with very few good dining spots. She and her husband Dave wanted to do it right, so they bought a plot of land about a block from the center of town and built a 4700 square foot two-story building that was finished early in 2007. They finished the project by professionally landscaping with raised flower beds and rose bushes. As a volunteer at a local day care center, Jo recognized that she could do more with her gift of hospitality and that was to serve the hungry travelers who visit the rustic area each year. Since Dave works in Columbus, Jo and her two daughters, Katie and Leah, have taken over the day to day responsibilities of the restaurant, which has a feel of a diner, but the taste of home, complete with fresh vegetables and herbs from the Eaves' garden and from the local farmers' market when in season. No frozen meat here, all steaks and chicken are shipped whole and custom cut for each guest.

This is not an inn where they have overnight guests, but Jo explained to me that the reason they chose the name Ridge Inn was because the restaurant is located at the corner of Route 56 and Thompson Ridge Road and they chose "inn" because they wanted to be unique from the other restaurants in town.

They serve three meals, seven days a week with great coffee. Breakfast goes beyond bacon and eggs, and features Biscuits and Gravy with fluffy homemade buttermilk biscuits and country sausage gravy. The Croissant French Toast starts with a flaky croissant that is dipped in a cinnamon egg batter and grilled to perfection. And don't forget the stacks and stacks of golden pancakes smothered with blueberries, cranberries, chocolate chips or pecans. Try one of Jo's mouthwatering homemade donuts, which has earned her a favorable reputation in the area. Wash it down with a cappuccino, latte, frappe or specialty tea.

Before I indulged in one of their specialties (meatloaf and smashed potatoes), I first tasted the Cusabi chicken salad, which was excellent. Cusabi dressing appears in many of their dishes and is a creamy sauce with a touch of horseradish that adds a just the right spark to the meat. And the slightly sweet corn nuggets are crunchy and something that most children would love. This is not only a place "where fine dining meets home cooking," but a place where families are welcome.

After a fine meal, check out the small gift shop in the back of the restaurant and, in season, the wide selection of handmade log furniture displayed on the front lawn.

DINERS INFORMATION

Address
16178 Pike St., Laurelville, OH 43135
www.theridgeinnrestaurant.com

Phone
(740) 332-0300

Hours
Monday - Thursday, 8:00 a.m. – 8:00 p.m.
Friday - Saturday, 8:00 a.m. – 9:00 p.m.
Sunday, 8:00 a.m. – 5:00 p.m.

Price Range
$

The Sandstone

Logan, OH

Located on Main Street in downtown Logan, this quiet restaurant provides a relaxing setting with delicious homemade specialties. At the time of my visit the main chef was a student from the Culinary Arts Department of nearby Hocking College located in Nelsonville who was nearing her graduation. She had learned her art and was well trained at this highly regarded school known for turning out professional chefs. She provided me with a sampling of the house specialties that included a thick and tasty Spinach and Artichoke Dip that brimmed with chunks of artichokes and garlic and was served with home made toasted Parmesan Herb French bread, just perfect to capture large bites of the dip. The Blackened Chicken Alfredo featured delicate homemade linguine noodles in a thick creamy sauce topped with thinly sliced chicken. The Three Cheese Au Gratin is a classic French onion soup topped with a slice of sour dough bread and a bubbly blend of three cheeses (Swiss, mozzarella and provolone). If you like seafood another delicious specialty is the Shrimp and Scallop Sambuca that features sautéed Sea Scallops and Tiger Shrimp in a Sambuca liqueur served over rice. The menu also offers the more adventurous diner an opportunity to build his or her own pizza or burger from scratch, selecting whatever items that suit his/her taste.

Only certified Angus beef is provided, along with fresh seafood and poultry, local produce in season and fresh bread daily. A full bar with fine wine, spirits and

a variety of beer is available as well as nonalcoholic drinks.

A well kept secret, at least to me, was The Sandstone Patio located behind the main restaurant with a separate entrance from the side street. It is just a laid back, great place to catch a burger, a wrap, Black Bean Dip or the Old Man's Cave Chicken Sandwich. Open from the first week in May, it closes when the weather changes in the fall.

This establishment has come a long way since its former sports bar days, and now provides casual fine dining with the prevailing theme dedicated to the Ohio canals. A large, detailed mural depicting the historic events that took place in the area was reputedly painted by local artist Don Phillips and graces the wall overlooking the dining area.

For a more informal atmosphere on warm summer nights, the patio is open with a full outside kitchen and bar. For those just passing through you can drop by and pick up your meal to go.

DINERS INFORMATION

?

Address
117 W. Main St., Logan, Ohio 43138
www.sandstonerestaurant.com

Phone
(740)-385-9479

Hours
Monday - Thursday, 4:00 p.m. – 8:00 p.m. (seasonal hours)
Friday - Saturday, 3:00 p.m. – 9:00 p.m.
Closed Sunday

Price Range
$$$

Zoe

Athens, OH

Located uptown Athens, this white tablecloth restaurant is quite a surprise in a college town, but it still has a comfortable casual elegance that makes dining there a pleasant and special experience. The owner and chef, Scott Bradley, had worked at Glenlaurel Inn and the Big Chimney Baking Company, and then opened a smaller scale of Zoe. Before long he moved to the current location where he not only expanded the seating, but the menu as well. His mission is to "provide Athens with the opportunity for high quality fine dining with professional service."

As the first steel and concrete reinforced building in Athens County, the East State Street structure was originally a brick manufacturing business. It eventually served as the local Greyhound bus station and then was turned into a nightclub. After it had been empty for a while, Scott thought it would be perfect for his new location so he painted and remodeled the interior, and kept the beautiful antique bar with the unique feature of hooks under the bar where women can hang their purses. The decor is upscale with muted lighting and a black and white color scheme. Though not a large restau-

rant, the floor plan is broken up to allow for intimate dining in relative privacy.

The ever-changing menu features Flatiron and Strip Steak, scallops, shrimp and salmon, duck, and chicken as well as vegetarian dishes with an emphasis on local, seasonal ingredients. The full bar features beer, mixed drinks and an international wine list.

I was served the Appetizer Trio that included a potato pancake with Portabella Relish, Risotto Cake with Artichoke lemon confit, and a Millet Fritter with hummus, all of which was excellent and made an appealing presentation. I also tried the Rabbit Sausage with Dijon mustard, garnished with watercress and I found it to be rather mild, but tasty. Next, I had the sautéed Skinned Duck Breast, which is served with Panko Crusted Shitake Rice Cakes and veggies in an orange soy ginger sauce. It was delicious with a delicate blend of sweet and tart taste. The Shrimp, Chicken and Artichoke Linguini is tossed with garlic, olive oil, roasted tomato, white wine and Romano cheese with a touch of cracked pepper. And the Roast Amish Chicken Breast with gnocchi is pan roasted and served over Asiago stuffed gnocchi with Shitaki mushrooms, tomatoes, spinach, Romano cheese and white wine cream. Authentic German Sauerbraten is also a popular dish. The tips of beef tenderloin are marinated in red wine and vinegar, braised and served in a rich sour German sauce over herb spaetzle with asparagus.

For dessert my favorite was Raspberry Crème Brulee, which is a rich custard made with local farm fresh eggs and whole raspberries, and topped with a crust of caramelized brown sugar. As an extra treat I tried the Baked Alaska, which was, as they say, "to die for." To clean the palette, I tasted the Mango and Raspberry Sorbet and quenched my thirst with green tea and honey. It certainly was a perfect ending to a delightful meal.

DINERS INFORMATION

Address
24 ½ East State Street, Athens, OH 45701
www.zoefinedining.com

Phone
(740) 592-4443

Hours
Tuesday - Saturday, 5:00 p.m. – 9:00 p.m.
Reservations recommended, but not required

Price Range
$$

About the Author

Karen A. Patterson earned a degree in communications from Marquette University before joining the National Safety Council in Chicago as an assistant editor. Writing became a passion and she embarked on a career in nonfiction writing.

Subsequently, she served as the editor for the National Eye Research Foundation, technical writer for Blue Cross Blue Shield in Chicago, director of communications for PricewaterhouseCoopers in Columbus, Ohio, and director for marketing and public relations for Adena Medical Center in Chillicothe, Ohio.

She transitioned into script writing and program development as the host of a Christian radio program on WCVO (104.9 FM) in Columbus, where she interviewed many accomplished writers and experts in health, nutrition and family issues from a Christian perspective. But after seven years, she left radio to teach in central Ohio colleges and universities.

Patterson completed a Masters in Fine Arts at Spalding University, specializing in nonfiction writing, and began working on her doctorate in Adult Education.

On the side, she continued to write and, as a certified master gardener, she produced a syndicated column for the Gannett and Thompson newspapers about the practical side of gardening. Her main focus, however, was raising and using herbs which resulted in her book, *Herbs for All Seasons*.

She has been recognized through a number of awards for the hundreds of articles that she has penned and the many books that she has either contributed to or authored. Her favorite is *Allies Forever: The Life and Times of an American Prisoner of War*, a memoir of her father who was shot down Christmas Day, 1944, and was held prisoner by the Germans.

On her life's journey, Patterson has travelled and tasted some of the finest food in the world in Israel, Africa, Nicaragua and the Caribbean, and written about her experiences in travel guides and articles. As a result Eating Across Ohio was a natural assignment for her.

In her spare time she enjoys being at home cooking up some exciting culinary creation and working in her herb gardens.

Patterson lives with her husband John in Chillicothe where they share four children, five grandchildren and even a few great-grandbabies.

Index